FAITH POWER

"it works better with all the parts"

By BILLY JOE DAUGHERTY

Unless otherwise indicated, all Scripture quotations in this volume are from the *King James Version* of the Bible.

ISBN 0-89274-100-7
Printed in the United States of America
Copyright © 1978 by Billy Joe Daugherty

BILLY JOE DAUGHERTY

Billy Joe Daugherty is pastor of Victory Christian Center in Tulsa, Oklahoma. A graduate of Oral Roberts University, he is called to take God's Word and ministry of the Spirit to this generation. His church has a Christian school and Bible institute to train students to be effective Christians.

Billy Joe's wife Sharon is an anointed singer and has recorded a number of albums. She ministers alongside her husband both in song and teaching.

Victory Christian School and Victory Bible Institute are training hundreds of students each year to be effective soldiers in God's army.

Victory Christian Center meets each Sunday in the ORU Mabee Center.

Table of Contents

Introduction

Many people are talking about faith. As we began to study the Word on this subject we could see that faith is made up of several components.

Faith is not solely believing. It is not simply confessing or just hearing the Word. Faith requires doing, yet that's not all. Although faith includes prayer, there is still more. Meditation is not the final answer either. Learning how to receive from God is a big part of faith too. Praise is powerful, but it needs to be supported by the other parts of faith.

In a given situation, a person may exercise great faith by utilizing only two or three parts of faith. This book is not a cut and dried formula that must be rigidly followed. It is a breakdown of faith that gives us an inner picture of how faith is developed and how it functions. The purpose is to teach the body of Christ how to develop and operate great faith by using everything God has given us.

We have been led by the Spirit to illustrate faith with the V-8 engine. The engine to the average onlooker is one machine. The person who knows engines, however, knows it is made up of many stationary and moving parts. Primarily, the engine itself has eight cylinders with pistons inside of them. Timed explosions in each of these cylinders causes power to be released to move the pistons. The moving pistons turn a shaft that harnesses the power from the explosion of the gasoline in the cylinder and eventually channels that power to turn the wheels.

Even though some of the pistons or cylinders are not functioning properly, the engine will still run—but it will be rough. It is the same with people and faith. Some people will get a lot of mileage out of half the parts of faith, but the full potential can only be reached by continuous exercise of all parts of faith. Jesus must be our example for He is the one person who developed His faith to perfection. Our faith will grow the same way and it will operate the same way, because it is His faith that we have been given.

The growth, development, and release of faith includes hearing the Word, believing the Word, praying according to the Word, receiving the promise, confessing the Word, meditating upon the Word. praising God, and doing the Word. You may think of other things that will help your faith as you read this book and God speaks to you personally.

1
Living By Faith

The phrase "the just shall live by faith" (Romans 1:17) appears four times in Scripture. God has given faith as the divine process of living in His Kingdom, with love as the single law. It is strong faith that enables us to enjoy a high standard of living in God's economy. Weak faith would not disqualify us from going to heaven, but it would drastically reduce the number of benefits we would enjoy and also decrease our usefulness to God in the work of His Kingdom.

All of God's provisions for an abundant life have been made available to the body of Christ. (John 10:10.) God guarantees to supply every need "according to his riches in glory by Christ Jesus" and His Word declares that He has already "blessed us with all spiritual blessings in heavenly places in Christ" (Philippians 4:19; Ephesians 1:3). Furthermore He has "given unto us all things that pertain unto life and godliness, through the knowledge of him that hath called us to glory and virtue" (II Peter 1:3).

God withholds no good thing "from them that walk uprightly" (Psalm 84:11). God's blessings are conditional; that is, we must obey Him and live in accordance with His standards if we expect to enjoy all His blessings. This does not mean that we can earn His blessings because they are the result of grace rather than the reward for service. The key is keeping our spirit, soul, and body in a state of seeking to please God through obedience and submission to His will, which is His Word. Jesus put it this way: "If ye abide in me, and my words abide in you, ye shall ask what ye will, and it shall be done unto you" (John 15:7).

It is clear from the Word of God that our Father wants to bless His children. But it is also clear that He intends for His children to bless Him and the rest of His family. It is marvelous to think about the fact that God has chosen us to work with Him and fulfill His purposes here on the earth. We are saved not only to be blessed but also to serve.

As we examine Ephesians 2:8-10, we will see that both our salvation and our works are by faith. "For by grace are ye saved through faith; and that not of yourselves: it is the gift of God: Not of works, lest any man should boast. For we are his workmanship, created in Christ Jesus unto good works, which God hath before ordained that we should walk in them."

God has already planned and prepared the good works we are to do. By faith we seek to obey God and do that which He has ordained for us to accomplish. Even though a man is saved and doing a multitude of good works, if those works are not by faith they will not please God.

"But without faith it is impossible to please him: for he that cometh to God must believe that he is, and that he is a rewarder of them that diligently seek him " (Hebrews 11:6).

The only way to live in the Kingdom of God is by faith. The only way to please God is by faith. The only way to recieve God's blessings is by faith. The only way to serve God is by faith.

I believe we could say faith working by love is important.

GOD IS NO RESPECTER OF PERSONS

God has chosen to love the world and He is not a respecter of persons. (John 3:16; Acts 10:34.) In His love God includes the unrighteous, the ungodly, the sinner, and whosoever will call upon the name of the Lord. (Romans 5:8; 10:13.)

ALL who accept Jesus can receive blessings and serve God. He has chosen to make His blessings and good works available to "whosoever will" on the basis of faith. Praise God!!!

You can be a blessing and you can receive blessings!

WHAT IS FAITH

"Now faith is the substance of things hoped for, the evidence of things not seen" (Hebrews 11:1). One translation of this verse reads, "Now faith is the title-deed of things hoped for"(Centenary translation). The Amplified version translates the second part of the verse "being the proof of things we do not see and the conviction of their reality-faith perceiving as real what is not revealed to the senses." Corrie ten Boom has said that faith is the radar that sees through the fog.*

Faith in God is faith in His Word. If God has given His Word concerning a certain issue, then we can trust Him to perform what He has spoken. His Word is the guaranty of the thing He has promised and it is just as good as the actual thing. If we put our faith in God's Word, we can rest assured that it will come to pass. It is so certain that God will not fail one of His promises that we can take His Word as the **evidence** of the very thing He has promised.

Amazing Love — Spire Books.

It is a great privilege to build our lives on a foundation that cannot be shaken and will stand firm against every wind, storm, and flood of the adversary. **Faith reaches for the eternal and brings it into existence in order to change the natural things.** You may be burdened with sin, sickness, discouragement, or confusion, but your faith in the eternal Word of God can overcome those feelings and give you victory in every situation. The temporal things will be changed by the Eternal, and you will be established on the Rock.

YOUR FAITH ENGINE

Your faith is very similar to the V-8 engine used in many cars. It is one operation, yet the power is generated through a series of operations within the engine itself. Each operation in faith has a specific place and will produce power if it is run by the Spirit. Although the engine may run on fewer than all 8 cylinders, its power and efficiency are greatly reduced. For highest performance every part of faith must be operating.

A car engine must be properly tuned and the timing set for it to run properly. Depending on the make and year of the car, the spark plugs and/or points must be firing with precision or the explosion of the gasoline-air mixture will not be good. Likewise, the pistons, valves, and cylinders need to be in good shape. If all these things are not in order, the engine will run rough, lack power, start poorly, and cause many problems. Are you getting the picture of why we are explaining the various parts of faith? If so much knowledge is needed just to run an automobile, why shouldn't we be more concerned about the great powerhouse God has given to us? Don't wait until a crisis arises to check your faith because it will be too late.

This book is really a tune-up manual for your faith. You may be operating all eight parts in faith and only need minor adjustments. It is necessary to study faith constantly because we need regular tune-ups. Plan now to check your faith regularly to insure continual high performance.

To make your tune-ups easier, we have dissected faith to examine each of the eight cycles individually. As we go on, you will see how these parts intermingle and support one another. Sometimes the Word of God will speak of two or three of these parts producing results. Then, in another passage of Scripture, there may be four or five parts of the faith process mentioned. It is by taking all of God's Word and placing these parts into one group that we begin to get the total picture.

Faith includes hearing, believing, praying, receiving, confessing, meditating, praising, and doing. All of these things are important, and you will probably discover other things that help our faith grow and mature to the place that it can be used to meet the needs of those around us. Remember, this is not a dead formula, a set of rules, or another do-it-yourself kit. It is a simple explanation of the various parts of faith using a modern parable.

Each one of the eight parts discussed in this book has been emphasized in the body of Christ. God has been tuning up our faith for a purpose: **the time is short and there are mountains to be moved.** We will need all the faith-power God has provided!

2

Faith Comes By Hearing God's Word

"So then faith cometh by hearing, and hearing by the word of God" (Romans 10:17). All our faith has come as a result of hearing God's Word. It is impossible to have faith in God apart from hearing His Word. Although we may have prayed for faith at some time in the past, it is a joy to discover that faith comes as a result of hearing the Word with an open heart thus enabling us to pray **with** faith rather than **for** it.

After a person hears the gospel of salvation, he has the faith to accept it if he is willing. If he believes, then he can pray a prayer of faith to be saved. "For whosoever shall call upon the name of the Lord shall be saved. How then shall they call on him in whom they have not believed? and how shall they believe in him of whom they have not heard? and how shall they hear without a preacher?" (Romans 10:13-14).

Here we see a combination of several of the parts of faith: hearing, believing, calling (confessing), and being saved (receiving).

Many prayers are seemingly unanswered because God's Word was not sought first. Faith in God can only come after we have heard His Word. If we know something is God's will because His Word declares it and it is established in the mouth of two or three witnesses, then faith can arise to believe, pray, receive, confess, meditate, praise and act.

FAITH FOR THE BAPTISM IN THE HOLY SPIRIT

Prior to my eighteenth birthday I had never heard much, if any, about the baptism in the Holy Spirit. I had no knowledge of the experience and consequently no desire or faith to receive the promise of the Father.

One day a friend shared the Scriptures with me about John prophesying that Jesus would baptize with the Holy Ghost. We looked into the book of Acts and he read how the 120 followers of Christ received this experience. I was thrilled to find out that God would give His power to common ordinary people. Realizing my own lack of spiritual power, I wanted the baptism of the Spirit.

Several weeks passed as I read the Scriptures concerning the infilling of the Spirit, and faith began to grow as I knew it was what God wanted for me. I came to the point that I knew God would bless me with the baptism in the Holy Spirit the moment I asked Him.

I did—He did—GLORY!—HALLELUJAH!

Jesus brought the miracle into my life.

SOWING THE WORD

Jesus told a parable of a sower who went into his field and began to sow seed for a crop. (Matthew 13:3-23.) Some of the seed fell by the way and was quickly eaten by the birds. Other seed fell on stony ground and sprang up immediately, but later it withered away under the scorching heat. Some seed fell among thorns and was choked by them. Finally some of the seed fell on good ground and produced some an hundredfold, some sixty, and some thirtyfold.

This parable concerns hearing the Word. Some people will lose even the little Word they hear while others will keep it but do not allow it to reach its full potential. **Remember this—the crop that is produced from the Word we hear depends on our attitude towards that Word.** The seed of God's Word has the same power to produce in any given life. The crop yield is determined by the preparation and cultivation of the ground along with the care and attention given to the crop from planting time to harvest. God will give the increase if we are willing and seeking.

Jesus said those who hear the Word but do not try to understand or keep it will have it snatched away by the devil. These are like the seed sown by the way-side and devoured by the birds.

Those who hear the Word and receive it at first but later are offended when tribulation and persecution arise, will let go of it. They are the seed sown on stony ground.

Folks who hear the Word, but put other things first such as business, pleasure, or worldly cares, will allow the Word to be choked out of their lives. These are like the seed sown among thorns.

"But he that received seed into the good ground is he that heareth the word, and understandeth it; which also beareth fruit, and bringeth forth, some an hundredfold, some sixty, some thirty" (Matthew 13:23).

If we are going to bring forth fruit in our faith, we must make an effort to really HEAR the Word. Jesus is talking not only about physical hearing, but primarily about spiritual hearing with the heart. Hearing with the heart requires a deep hunger and thirst to know God through His Word.

Our own human will, encouraged by the Spirit of God, determines the amount of fruit we will produce. Generally speaking, the fruit is faith in relation to the Word of God. Specifically, it could be faith for salvation, healing, love, joy, peace, victory or anything that God has promised in His Word. There are hundreds of promises in the Word of God for you.

Commit yourself to do, to be, and to receive all that God has planned for His new creation—that's you!

THE BEGINNING

"In the beginning was the Word, and the Word was with God, and the Word was God. And the Word was made flesh, and dwelt among us, (and we beheld his glory, the glory as of the only begotten of the Father,) full of grace and truth" (John 1:1, 14). Jesus and the Word are one. Positionally, Jesus is seated at the right hand of God, but at the same time He comes to us by His Word and Spirit here on earth. Jesus said, "the words that I speak unto you, they are spirit, and they are life" (John 6:63). Since the Holy Spirit was the author of the Word, the two always agree. (II Peter 1:20-21, I John 5:7-8.)

Everything we learn about Jesus will be through the Word. Whether it comes directly from the Spirit or through a minister, if it is about Jesus, then it will be consistent with the Word of God. **If it is not consistent with the whole counsel of God, then throw it out.**

Since faith comes through, by, and from Jesus, then faith comes through, by and from hearing the Word. If you want to enjoy the blessings of divine health and long life, then begin to search the Word of God in these areas. Whether it is protection, provision, or inner peace, it will come through the Word if it comes from God.

Some people wait until a crisis arises before they begin to seek God for help. No smart frontiersman would ever have waited until a blizzard hit before he chopped his firewood. In the same manner, our preparation in faith should be done now, ahead of time, before a storm hits. Jesus said those who build their house on the rock and those who build on the sand will both encounter storms, but only those on the rock will endure. He said those who build on the rock are the ones who hear and do His Word. (Matthew 7:24-27.)

DO NOT FEAR. Those who prepare now by fortifying their faith will stand victorious even in these last days. The world may be shaken and changed, but God's Kingdom will never be shaken. It is forever.

A crop is produced after seed is sown. Do not be discouraged if you do not have an overcoming faith attitude immediately. Remember, seed takes time to sprout, grow and then produce. **Be diligent in continually sowing God's Word in your heart.** Soon you will see "the blade, then the ear, after that the full corn in the ear" (Mark 4:28).

ATTEND TO GOD'S WORD

The book of Proverbs gives us some great instruction on how to hear God's Word. Listen to the Father speak to His children.

"My son, if thou wilt receive my words, and hide my commandments with thee; So that thou incline thine ear unto wisdom, and apply thine heart to understanding; Yea, if thou criest after knowledge, and liftest up thy voice for understanding; If thou seekest her as silver, and searchest for her as for hid treasures; Then shalt thou understand the fear of the Lord, and find the knowledge of God" (Proverbs 2:1-5).

Several action verbs are used to describe how we should hear God's Word. God tells us to RECEIVE His Words, HIDE His commandments, INCLINE our ears, APPLY our hearts, CRY after knowledge, LIFT up our voice, SEEK as for silver, and SEARCH as for treasure.

God wants us to know and understand that this business of hearing His Word is important. It will take genuine effort and dedication, but the harvest will be worth it all. God, in His grace, will bring us to the completion He desires.

HEARING THE GOSPEL BROUGHT FAITH FOR HEALING

Paul came to a city called Lystra and began to preach the gospel of Jesus Christ. "And there sat a certain man at Lystra, impotent in his feet, being a cripple from his mother's womb, who never had walked: The same heard Paul speak: who stedfastly beholding him, and perceiving that he had faith to be healed, Said with a loud voice, Stand upright on thy feet. And he leaped and walked" (Acts 14:8-10).

Paul was preaching the gospel of Jesus Christ to the group. The gospel, or good news, of salvation according to Paul clearly included physical healing. Not only could sins be forgiven and men's spirits be reborn, but also sicknesses could be removed and bodies healed.

Notice the man "heard" Paul speak. The entrance of God's Word brought light. (Psalm 119:130.) Faith reached out of his heart and laid hold of the wonderful words of life. The miracle was completed as he acted on what he had heard. **Faith came by hearing the Word.**

3

Believing God

"Jesus said unto him, If thou canst believe, all things are possible to him that believeth" (Mark 9:23).

Our believing is greatly influenced by our thinking. Right thinking will produce right believing. Right thinking begins with KNOWING God's Word. Our thinking and consequently our believing is shaped by what we hear. Therefore, it is imperative to hear words of faith if we want to have faith. Listening to doubt, negativism and idle talk can neutralize our ability to believe.

Jesus tells us right believing can open up for us the impossible. This means we must not only hear God's Word, but also believe it. Believing God is believing His Word. Trusting God is trusting what He has spoken through the Scriptures.

BASIS FOR BELIEVING GOD

Before we can believe God's Word, we must be sure that His Word can be trusted. Does the Bible actually contain God's will? Is it truly inspired? Thank God, yes it is! "All scripture is given by inspiration of God, and is profitable for doctrine, for reproof, for correction, for instruction in righteousness; That the man of God may be perfect, throughly furnished unto all good works" (II Timothy 3:16-17).

Because the Word of God is inspired, it is just as powerful today as it was when it was spoken. The

Word of God endures forever. (I Peter 1:25.) It will still be operating when time ceases. "For the word of God is quick, and powerful . . ." (Hebrews 4:12.)

"God is not a man, that he should lie; neither the son of man, that he should repent: hath he said, and shall he not do it? or hath he spoken, and shall he not make it good?" (Numbers 23:19.)

His Word has been tried as silver in a furnace, purified seven times. (Psalm 12:6.) God said what He meant and meant what He said. We should never try to change God's Word to fit our denominational doctrines or past traditions. **Rather, we should align our doctrine and lifestyle with God's inspired Word.**

Even though the Word of God came through human beings, its inspiration is not diminished in any way. It even becomes more relevant to our lives when we realize God used people like us to speak and record His Word.

"Knowing this first, that no prophecy of the scripture is of any private interpretation. For the prophecy came not in old time by the will of man: but holy men of God spake as they were moved by the Holy Ghost" (II Peter 1:20-21).

Believing God is easier when we recognize the divine inspiration of His Word. We can trust the whole weight of our faith on God's Word because He has promised that it will not return to Him void, but will accomplish that which He pleases, and it will prosper in the thing whereto He sent it. (Isaiah 55:11.)

PERSONAL CHILD-LIKE BELIEVING

Jesus said, "Except ye be converted, and become as little children, ye shall not enter into the kingdom of heaven" (Matthew 18:3). A young child that has not heard lies will simply take her parents at their word. The little one believes everything mommy or daddy says. Doubt has not entered in yet because of the simplicity of life. For small children faith comes easy. If daddy keeps his word from the start, the young one will believe anything he promises.

Our heavenly Father has never lied. He has never failed to keep and fulfill His Word. We can be just like little children and take our Father at His Word. It will please the Father to see us acting as youngsters, believing His Word. (Hebrews 11:6.)

Sometimes we may hear or read the Word of God and think about how much someone else needs to apply that command or promise. We must take heed to ourselves to appropriate God's commands and blessings for our own lives. God's Word is for you and me to apply personally in our lives.

One night, in a West Texas town, I preached on seeking God and laying our lives down to do service for Him. A man spoke to me after it was over and said, "If they'd a been here, you'd a told 'em off right." Somehow, I think he missed the point of my message.

SIN OF UNBELIEF

"Take heed, brethren, lest there be in any of you an evil heart of unbelief, in departing from the living God" (Hebrews 3:12).

This passage of Scripture compares the children of Israel with Christians today. Just as God promised Israel a land of rest, flowing with milk and honey, He promised His children today an abundant life as partakers of Christ.

The first time Israel reached the edge of Canaan, God instructed them to send in twelve spies to survey the land. Ten of the spies returned telling of the land's bounty; but then they began to tell of the strong people, walled cities and giants in the land. Joshua and Caleb, the other two spies, began to encourage the people to go up immediately and possess the land saying they were able to overcome it. (Numbers 13:26-33.)

The sin of Israel was unbelief, at this point. God had promised to give them the land, but they would not go in and possess it. Instead of believing the faith report, they accepted the doubt message. They began to murmur and the whole congregation said to Moses and Aaron, ". . . Would God that we had died in the land of Egypt! or would God we had died in this wilderness" (Numbers 14:2).

Because of the hardness of their hearts, God gave them their request instead of His promise. He told them, "Your carcasses shall fall in this wilderness; and all that were numbered of you, according to your whole number, from twenty years old and upward, which have murmured against me" (Numbers 14:29). Exactly as God said, those people perished in the wilderness in the following years. Only Joshua and Caleb lived to enter the promised land at the end of the 40 years in the wilderness.

Many good people have failed to enter the promised land because they focused their eyes on the circumstances rather than on God's Word. Take the attitude of believing God no matter what comes. God calls unbelief sin, or evil. **It is a sin to doubt the integrity and ability of God's Word.** However, there is nothing wrong with searching the Word to discover its true meaning. In other words, we could say, "Lord, I definitely believe your Word; so could you just show me for sure what your Word is saying?"

Unbelief causes a person to depart from the living God. To draw back from faith is to draw back from God. "Without faith it is impossible to please him . . ." (Hebrews 11:6). Believing God for **all** His promises is a must. We do not have an option to pick and choose.

"Let us therefore fear, lest, a promise being left us of entering into his rest, any of you should seem to come short of it, For unto us was the gospel preached, as well as unto them: but the word preached did not profit them, not being mixed with faith in them that heard it" (Hebrews 4:1-2).

We should have a holy fear of God that would motivate us to receive everything God has promised for us in His Word. It is not enough just to hear the gospel. **We must mix our faith with the Word.** It is a joyful privilege to have all our needs met in Jesus. Truly it is a faith rest. (Hebrews 4:9-12.)

ABRAHAM BELIEVED GOD

"Abraham believed God, and it was counted unto him for righteousness" (Romans 4:3). God promised Abram He would bless him and that through him all the families of the earth would be blessed. He told him to leave his own country and kindred to go into another land. (Genesis 12:1-4.) Abram believed God and obeyed His Word.

Twenty-five years passed and God spoke again to Abram whose name He had changed to Abraham. He confirmed His promise that Sarah would give birth to a son. The idea of a baby sounded funny to 100-year-old Abraham and 90-year-old Sarah. They laughed. But God had the last laugh—Isaac was born within a year. In spite of the laughter, Abraham believed God would perform His Word.

"And being not weak in faith, he considered not his own body now dead, when he was about an hundred years old, neither yet the deadness of Sarah's womb; He staggered not at the promise of God through unbelief; but was strong in faith, giving glory to God; And being fully persuaded that, what he had promised, he was able also to perform. And therefore it was imputed to him for righteousness" (Romans 4:19-22).

Abraham had to believe God when there was no hope from the natural standpoint. The Bible says he did not stagger at God's promise. In other words, he did not waver. He had fixed his heart to the point of being fully persuaded that God would perform His Word. The end result of believing God was imputed righteousness. Abraham's unwavering faith caused God to reckon him, or credit him, with righteousness in the eyes of divine justice.

ONLY BELIEVE

The only way to know if you really believe God's Word or not, is to act upon it. You see, to believe is to put total confidence or trust in what God has spoken. Believing with the heart is not mental assent and mental assent is not believing, for sure. Mental assent would say, "I know God's Word is true, but it's just not for me right now." On the contrary, a believer says, "I am going to act on God's Word because I believe it in my heart, no matter what my mind tries to tell me." **The believer will eventually renew his mind to know God's will and think accordingly.**

There is a definite battle to win over common sense in the faith walk. God's Word and man's words are contrary to one another until man begins to submit to God. Nothing God does or says makes sense to the natural man. (I Corinthians 2:14.)

If you try to use common sense, you will get the same common results that all the rest of the common people get. Why not "set your affection on things above" (Colossians 3:2), and live as God has planned for you by believing His Word instead of what everyone else says. You will find that every Word that proceeds from the mouth of God is life. (Matthew 4:4.)

4

Praying

A very important part in our faith is prayer. We could think of prayer in many ways but we will primarily discuss it along the line of **petition, supplication,** and **request to change circumstances.** The Word tells us to "pray without ceasing, continue in prayer, watch unto prayer, and always pray" (I Thessalonians 5:17, Colossians 4:2, Ephesians 6:18).

GROWING FAITH

Prayer is the release of what we hear and believe. It is to the spirit what exercise is to the body. Continual prayer that gets results will cause our faith to mature. Prayer uses the Word that has come to the heart and releases faith for that Word in the form of a petition to God. It is this continual process that develops faith.

"We are bound to thank God always for you, brethren, as it is meet, because that your faith growth exceedingly, and the charity of every one of you all toward each other aboundeth" (II Thessalonians 1:3).

Never be satisfied with mediocre faith. **Faith is a commodity that is either increasing or decreasing.** Rarely does a person ever stand still in faith. If we were in an opposition-free world, we could suppose that a person might turn off his faith for a while and it would remain in the same place. But, there is an adversary in the world that does not stop and rest when Christians relax their faith. Faith is a rest, but it must be constantly exercised and fed, to grow and mature.

The exertion of our will to continually **hear** God's Word, **believe** every bit of it, and **pray** accordingly, is the force needed to keep faith growing. Sometimes you may have to tell yourself to start praying. God's Spirit will move us, but we must be willing and yielded.

REST

"There remaineth therefore a rest to the people of God. For he that is entered into his rest, he also hath ceased from his own works, as God did from his. Let us labour therefore to enter into that rest, lest any man fall after the same example of unbelief" (Hebrews 4:9-11).

The prayer life is actually two-sided. In prayer, we fight the good fight of faith, and at the same time, we rest ourselves in God, trusting Him to accomplish His Word. **Real faith is both a fight and a rest.** Yes, we do battle with spiritual wickedness. But, praise God, the battle is the Lord's. (II Chronicles 20:15.)

As we receive righteousness by faith, we come into a place of confidence in our prayer life. "The effectual fervent prayer of a righteous man availeth much" (James 5:16). Our prayer life is powerful—it changes situations. We stand calm, in a place of rest. We know God is for us, who could come against us and win? (Romans 8:31.)

"And the work of righteousness shall be peace; and the effect of righteousness quietness and assurance for ever" (Isaiah 32:17). We are resting in God's strength, ability, and wisdom. We believe that no weapon formed against us shall prosper. (Isaiah 54:17.) In fact, we are prospering in whatever we do. (Psalm 1:1-3.)

THE GROWING WORD

After Peter and John ministered healing to a lame man, they met with opposition from the religious leaders. (Acts 3,4.) Because of the situation, the disciples and the believers gathered for prayer.

"And when they had prayed the place was shaken where they were assembled together; and they were all filled with the Holy Ghost, and they spake the word of God with boldness" (Acts 4:31).

Fervent prayer caused the disciples to begin speaking the Word with a greater power. The Holy Ghost was there all the time but it was not until they prayed that He filled them with boldness. Signs and wonders began to follow and confirm the Word. Notice that it was prayer that opened the believers to receive the boldness of the Holy Ghost which, in turn, caused them to speak the Word.

As the Word grew, the message of Christ was growing, and Christ was growing in the believers. "And the word of God increased; and the number of disciples multiplied in Jerusalem greatly" (Acts 6:7). **Churches interested in growth should study these scriptures.**

"But the word of God grew and multiplied" (Acts 12:24). As seed sown in the ground, so the Word sown in the heart will not just be doubled, but multiplied.

"So mightily grew the word of God and prevailed". (Acts 19:20.) Here is our destination. First, the Word comes to us in power. It begins to increase and grow. Next, it multiplies and finally Jesus, the Word, prevails over, in, and through us. Glory!

ASK IN PRAYER

Although God knows our needs before we ask Him, we are instructed to ask for these needs to be met.

(Matthew 6:8.) "And all things, whatsoever ye shall
ask in prayer, believing, ye shall receive" (Matthew
21:22).

Notice the Word says **all things**. Contrary to po-
pular opinion, God intends for us to receive **all
things** we pray for. Jesus makes this statement without apology several times in Scripture. You may be
asking the question, "why do so many not receive
answers then?" Certainly it is not God's fault if we
do not receive those things He has promised to us.
Therefore, the problems must come from self or the
devil, or both.

God has set up divine principles and methods
for prayer. Over and over again, the Word declares
we can receive through prayer, "all things, whatsoever things we desire, whatsoever we ask, anything,
and what we will" (Matthew 21:22; Mark 11:24; John
16:23, 14:13, 15:7). If we fail to receive, it could pos-
sibly be a result of failure to follow God's principles, methods, and directions. A common expression
says, "When all else fails, read the instructions."
Thank God, we can forget the past sins, get into the
manual (Word), and plan for success.

ASK THE FATHER IN JESUS' NAME

It may seem elementary, but when you ask, be
sure to ask the right One, using the right Name. Jesus
said, "And in that day ye shall ask me nothing. Verily,
verily, I say unto you, Whatsoever ye shall ask the
Father in my name, he will give it to you" (John 16:23).

Jesus tells us, specifically, to **pray to the Father in
His name.** Our Father honors the name of Jesus, above
all names. To use the name of Jesus is one of the
greatest privileges we have in our Christian life. His
name is the key to opening up the prayer line. If you

say you are calling for mercy in Jesus' name, the Father will hear your prayer.

"Hitherto have ye asked nothing in my name: ask and ye shall receive, that your joy may be full" (John 16:24).

Answered prayer always brings joy.

We know that we are co-laborers together with God through answered prayers. He directs our prayers and consequently, we pray according to His directions. He answers and we shout for joy! We even have joy the moment we pray because Jesus tells us, "What things soever ye desire, when ye pray, believe that ye receive them, and ye shall have them" (Mark 11:24).

If we receive by faith the moment we pray, then joy can be ours before the actual thing comes into physical existence. We already have it by faith. It is ours because we checked with God's Word at the start and determined it was God's will for us. Go ahead and rejoice! Keep your eyes on Jesus, for He is the author and finisher of our faith.

ACCORDING TO HIS WILL

"Ye ask, and receive not, because ye ask amiss, that ye may consume it upon your lusts" (James 4:3).

Jesus said that we could receive what soever things we desire. (Mark 11:24.) Some have failed to realize the difference between spiritual desire and carnal desire. Spiritual desire springs from the heart of the recreated being in fellowship with the heavenly Father. Carnal desire springs from the lusts of the mind and flesh that are fellowshipping with the evil one or the world system.

Jesus has given us the plan for cultivating spiritual desire, according to His will. It is called "Abiding in the vine." (John 15:1-5.)

He has promised us, "If ye abide in me, and my words abide in you, ye shall ask what ye will, and it shall be done unto you" (John 15:7).

The entrance of the Word of God brings light into our spirit, soul, and body. (Psalm 119:130.) This light is powerful. "For the word of God is quick and powerful, and sharper than any two-edged sword, piercing even to the diving asunder of soul and spirit, and of the joints and marrow, and is a discerner of the thoughts and intents of the heart. Neither is there any creature that is not manifest in his sight; but all things are naked and opened unto the eyes of him with whom we have to do" (Hebrews 4: 12-13).

As we abide in the Word, God will reveal to us His desires. We will be able to differentiate between spirit, soul, and body. Nothing can be hidden from the powerful light of God's Word. Many fail in prayer because they never get to the point of studying God's Word, much less abiding in it. (II Timothy 2:15.)

The **first** thing to do before praying, is **settle God's will in your heart.** To find God's will, you must search His Word. God's Word is His will. His will is His Word. God does not say one thing and will another. Neither does He establish His will and speak contrary to it. God says what He wills, and His will is what He says.

God's Word tells us to establish every word in the mouth of two or three witnesses. (II Corinthians 13:1, Deuteronomy 19:15.) This is to keep us from taking one word and being misled. Most error in Christianity has resulted from a truth taken out of context or blown out of proportion to God's original intention.

We want to take the whole counsel of God to establish God's will. The entire Word is God's will; yet His will concerning a specific area, may not be given entirely in one passage. Therefore, we must build our doctrines by comparing Scripture throughout the Bible.

"For precept must be upon precept, precept upon precept; line upon line, line upon line; here a little and there a little" (Isaiah 28:10).

Quite a bit of Jesus' teaching came from various places in the books which we now call the Old Testament. His Sermon on the Mount includes portions of verses from Psalms, I and II Chronicles, Exodus, Deuteronomy, Leviticus, I Kings, Isaiah, and II Samuel— to mention a few. Although the Scriptures had been written hundreds of years earlier, Jesus evidently considered them valid for His day and time. The reason for this, of course, is that God's Word is eternal.

"All scripture is given by inspiration of God, and is profitable for doctrine, for reproof, for correction, for instruction in righteousness" (II Timothy 3:16).

As we establish God's will from His Word, we can rest assured that His Word is accurate. It will not fail us as we base our prayers on it. Furthermore, we can be assured God will hear us when we are asking according to His will. And if He hears us, we know that He will give it to us.

"And this is the confidence that we have in him, that, if we ask anything according to his will, he heareth us: And if we know that he hear us, whatsoever we ask we know that we have the petitions that we desired of him" (I John 5:14-15).

FIX YOUR HEART AND MIND

Once we determine God's will by seeking Him through His Word and Spirit, then we set the desire of our heart and mind upon that will. This is of utmost importance in prayer because there may be storms, floods, and winds to hit us before we see the answer manifested.

Here is what the Word says about double-mindedness.

"If any of you lack wisdom, let him ask of God, that giveth to all men liberally, and upbraideth not; and it shall be given him. But let him ask in faith, nothing wavering. For he that wavereth is like a wave of the sea driven with the wind and tossed. For let not that man think that he shall receive anything of the Lord. A double-minded man is unstable in all his ways" (James 1:5-8).

What a terrible situation: tossed to and fro with every wave of the enemy. Take heed and search out God's will concerning the important areas of life and godliness.

Settle the Word now in your mind.

At the same time we are renewing our mind to the truth of God's Word, we should establish our heart. The heart fixed on God's Word will generate life from the inside out. "He shall not be afraid of evil tidings: his heart is fixed, trusting in the Lord. His heart is established, he shall not be afraid, until he sees his desire upon his enemies" (Psalm 112:7-8).

Begin now to **fix** your heart, **settle** your mind, and **submit** your body to the divine will of God's Word. The power in your prayer life will begin to **grow** and **show**.

MAINTAIN RIGHTEOUSNESS

The moment we receive Christ as our Savior, we receive the gift of righteousness. (Romans 10:8-10.) God has made provision for us to stay cleansed from all unrighteousness. "If we confess our sins, he is faithful and just to forgive us our sins and to cleanse us from all unrighteousness" (I John 1:9). The idea of righteousness is important in prayer because it is the "effectual, fervent prayer of a righteous man" that gets results. (James 5:16.)

"For the eyes of the Lord are over the righteous, and his ears are open unto their prayers: but the face of the Lord is against them that do evil" (I Peter 3:12).

This principle is often neglected because it requires Christians to examine themselves and repent of impure thoughts, deeds, words, and motives. I am personally thankful for this principle because it is just one more encouragement to live a holy, pure life before God and man.

Let me repeat: **Faith will deteriorate where there is continual sin without repentance.**

"Beloved, if our heart condemn us not, then have we confidence toward God. And whatsoever we ask, we receive of him, because we keep his commandments, and do those things that are pleasing in his sight" (I John 3:21-22).

5

Receiving From God

Receiving means accepting or taking. The Word of God tells us to receive by faith the thing we pray for, at the very moment we pray. "Therefore I say unto you, whatsoever things ye desire, when ye pray, believe that ye receive them, and ye shall have them" (Mark 11:24).

God wants us to trust Him to the point of actually receiving from Him **before** we see or feel anything. "Faith is the evidence of things not seen" (Hebrews 11:1). Faith will say, "I have it because I believe I have received according to God's Word." Doubt will say, "I will believe it when I see it." Faith takes God at His Word; doubt wants evidence it can see or feel.

RECEIVING CHRIST

"But as many as received him, to them gave he power to become the sons of God, even to them that believe on his name" (John 1:12).

At the time of our salvation, we received God's Word into our heart **by faith.** A faith image was formed as we pictured the Spirit of Christ entering our heart as the Word promised. This receiving was spiritual at first, rather than physical. To the natural senses there may have been no visible changes, yet the eye of faith saw the life of Jesus coming inside to the inner man. At the time, we probably did not understand all of the theological terms, but from what we had heard, we knew Jesus was coming inside us.

All of God's promises should be treated in this same manner. As we pray according to what we believe, our faith receives the promise from God, first of all, into our spirit. Then our mind is filled with thoughts of the promise until it is renewed by the Word. There may be no visible changes outwardly at first, but we know we have received God's promise into our heart and it will be fulfilled in the natural.

The principle of receiving by faith is very important. Without first establishing the Word in your heart, your confession will not carry any power. The Word believed and received into your heart will give your confession authority.

The psalmist wrote of the unmoveable man. At the very root of a steadfast Christian is the fixed heart. "He shall not be afraid of evil tidings: his heart is fixed, trusting in the Lord" (Psalm 112:7). The **heart is fixed** by receiving God's promises by faith and refusing to let go.

LOOKING AT THE UNSEEN

"While we look not at the things which are seen, but at the things which are not seen: for the things which are seen are temporal; but the things which are not seen are eternal" (II Corinthians 4:18).

The physical world and all that it involves is only temporal, or subject to change. Conditions as they look and feel are only temporary. However, God has given us faith in His eternal Word to use in changing temporal conditions.

"For we walk by faith, not by sight" (II Corinthians 5:7). Walking by faith gives us a continual sense of confidence. We know that God has spoken and His Word will endure after all that is temporal has vanished away. In order to walk by faith and not sight, **we must receive God's Word as the evidence** of what we may not sense with the five physical senses.

MIX THE WORD WITH FAITH

"Let us therefore fear, lest, a promise being left us of entering into his rest, any of you should seem to come short of it. For unto us was the gospel preached, as well as unto them: but the word preached did not profit them, not being mixed with faith in them that heard it" (Hebrews 4:1-2).

When Moses led the children of Israel out of Egypt, it did not take a long time for the group to reach the promised land. Although God had given them the land to possess, they did not mix faith with His promise. Therefore, they refused to believe the Word and enter the land. This cost all of the men, twenty years and older, their lives as they returned to wander in the wilderness.

Before you can receive the Word into your heart, you must believe it. But even though you may believe that God's Word is true, it will not work for you until you receive it personally and act upon it. As you can see, the different parts of faith are so closely linked that they must operate together in most instances. Remember, we are only dividing the different parts of faith to give us a better understanding of how faith comes, matures, and acts.

The writer of Hebrews uses the account of Israel in the wilderness to explain how faith is to be mixed with the Word of God. It is similar to a chemical reaction caused by the uniting of two substances. Apart from each other, the substances may be inactive; yet when they come together, a reaction takes place.

God's Word can be heard, but without mixing it with faith, it can be inactive as far as the individual is concerned. On the other hand, **when faith reaches out to believe and receive the Word, a powerful force is created that is strong enough to move mountains!**

BARTIMAUS RECEIVED BY FAITH

Blind Bartimaus sat by the highway begging until he heard that Jesus was coming his way. Then he began to cry out, "Jesus, thou Son of David, have mercy on me" (Mark 10:46-52).

"And Jesus answered and said unto him, What wilt thou that I should do unto thee? The blind man said unto him, Lord, that I might receive my sight."

Notice, Bartimaus had already **determined what he wanted to receive from Jesus.** His thoughts were **centered** more **on receiving** what he needed than the fact of his blindness. This may seem trivial, but it is a detriment to faith for us to be so engrossed with the problem that we cannot concentrate on the ANSWER. Bartimaus had fixed his mind and heart on receiving his sight.

Receiving from God requires an attitude of expectancy in accord with the promises of the Word. Bartimaus told Jesus what he expected to receive. Notice Jesus' response to Bartimaus.

"And Jesus said unto him, Go thy way; thy faith hath made thee whole. And immediately he received his sight, and followed Jesus in the way."

Jesus healed people through various methods, but in this case, He merely acknowledged to Bartimaus that his faith had made him whole. Jesus granted his desire **on the basis of faith,** and because it was in the will of God. Bartimaus received what he requested.

WHAT WE CAN RECEIVE

The first step in receiving from God by faith is to find out what God wants us to have. Praise the Lord! God has made His will available to us in the form of His Word.

God's will is to save the lost people of the world. (John 3:16-17.)

His will is to free men completely. (John 8:36.)

His will is to bind up and heal. (Luke 4:18.)

His will is abundant life. (John 10:10.)

His will is for His children to love Him and each other. (Matthew 22:37-39.)

There are many more Scriptures confirming each one of these specific areas of God's will. As you can easily see, God is not trying to hide His will from the body of Christ. On the contrary, He is doing everything He can to let us know His will. (I Corinthians 2:9-12, John 8:32.)

AFTER establishing God's will, then it is time to believe, pray, and receive. Receiving by faith is much easier if we are fully assured of God's will and desire, from the Word. If God desires for us to have something and has made provision for us to have it, then basically our job in prayer is to take our Father at His Word and tell Him what we need. The same goes for doing what the Word tells us. If God tells us to do something, then it can be done. We can receive it with joy because we know it can be fulfilled by the grace of God.

There must be an attitude both of humility and confidence as we approach God. Realizing that pride and self-exaltation were satan's downfall, we keep ourselves in a humbled state before God. Yet, we are confident that God accepts us on the basis of Jesus' sacrifice. As our high priest, He is seated at the Father's right hand and gives us an open invitation to come boldly into the throne room.

Humble yourself, yet be confident in Chirst. KEEP THE BALANCE.

SIMPLE FAITH

We have a young friend who learned early how to receive from God. At about age 12, he went to services and heard the Word of God taught in the area of faith. Tapes of the messages were available on cassette, but he had neither a cassette player nor enough money to buy one. He prayed at the first of the week's meeting and asked God to somehow give him a cassette player.

Our friend had heard enough of the Word to know he should act as if he already had the player. Since he had the player by faith, all he needed were the messages which cost $1 each, at the time. With the few dollars he had in his bank, he began to purchase a tape each night.

We did not hear the story until the end of the week. We discovered that no one but his parents knew what he was doing. But **faith can move God** to speak to someone who does not even know the need. This is what happened: at the end of the week, someone gave him a new cassette player.

ASK AND RECEIVE

Jesus speaks to us today in the same way He spoke nearly 2,000 years ago. "Hitherto have ye asked nothing in my name: ask, and ye shall receive, that your joy may be full" (John 16:24).

It is simple child-like faith that gets the job done. We believe we receive when we pray. (Mark 11:24.)

6

Confession

There are several phrases that could be used to describe this part of the faith process. It could be **the things we say** or speak, **the words of our mouth, our conversation, the fruit of our lips, our tongue, mouth,** or **lips.** All of these words and phrases give us a better idea of what we mean by the word confession.

James says the tongue is like a bit in the mouth of the horse, or like the rudder on a ship. Although it is small it can control and direct our lives.

"Behold, we put bits in the horses' mouths, that they may obey us; and we turn about their whole body. Behold also the ships, which though they be so great, and are driven of fierce winds, yet are they turned about with a very small helm, whithersoever the governor listeth. Even so the tongue is a little member, and boasteth great things" (James 3:3-5).

The Word says no man can tame the tongue. But we know Jesus can! **The tongue, if it is not tamed, can destroy a life.** "It is an unruly evil, full of deadly poison. And the tongue is a fire, a world of iniquity: so is the tongue among our members, that it defileth the whole body, and setteth on fire the course of nature; and it is set on fire of hell" (James 3:8,6).

The confession of our mouth is important to put the fire out, especially since the fire originates in hell. We must make an all-out effort to let Jesus tame our tongue before it runs the ship of our lives into dangerous waters. **The key is speaking God's Word.**

MOUTH REVEALS HEART

As Jesus condemned the Pharisees, He unveiled the connection between the heart and mouth.

"O generation of vipers, how can ye, being evil, speak good things? for out of the abundance of the heart the mouth speaketh. A good man out of the good treasure of the heart bringeth forth good things: and an evil man out of the evil treasure bringeth forth evil things. But I say unto you, That every idle word that men shall speak, they shall give account thereof in the day of judgment. For by thy words thou shalt be justified, and by thy words thou shalt be condemned" (Matthew 12: 34-37).

The mouth will speak in accord with the fulness of the heart, either good or evil. Consequently, Jesus said we would give account even for the idle words. Why not? These are the ones that most often come directly from the heart, by-passing the mind.

It is remarkable that Jesus said our justification or condemnation would depend **on our words**. Yet, this is consistent with the plan of salvation by faith given in the book of Romans.

"But what saith it? The word is nigh thee, even in thy mouth, and in thy heart: that is, the word of faith, which we preach; That if thou shalt confess with thy mouth the Lord Jesus, and shalt believe in thine heart that God hath raised him from the dead, thou shalt be saved. For with the heart man believeth unto right-eousness; and with the mouth confession is made unto salvation" (Romans 10:8-10).

It is the Word of faith that we are to believe and speak. The Word of faith is "Jesus is my Lord." The belief is "I believe God raised Jesus from the dead."

The moment we believe and speak the Word, we receive the promise. (Notice the interworking of the faith parts—it does not always go in the same pattern.)

The two steps of believing and speaking operate continually in our faith. If God's Word says it, we can believe and speak it also. Remember, it must be established by two or three witnesses and be consistent with the whole counsel of God. (II Corinthians 13:1; Acts 20:27.) Our belief and confession will then have the solid backing and foundation of God.

DEATH AND LIFE IN THE TONGUE

"A man's belly shall be satisfied with the fruit of his mouth; and with the increase of his lips shall he be filled. Death and life are in the power of the tongue: and they that love it shall eat the fruit thereof " (Proverbs 18:20-21).

The wisdom of God says we will enjoy things after our mouth has spoken them. Actually, we receive what we are believing and confessing. If we are believing and speaking words of life, we will "eat the fruit thereof" and enjoy abundant life. In the same way, words of death produce the things of death.

Abundant life includes salvation, health, freedom, power, joy, love, peace, victory, light, prosperity, kindness, gentleness, hope, faith and many other beautiful things.

To show the contrast, sin and death include doom, gloom, fear, doubt, worry, tension, strife, sickness, poverty, confusion and bondage—to name a few.

The power of life and death is in your tongue. **Begin now to believe, speak and enjoy God's life.** You may not see all these things physically, at first, but they belong to you legally and your faith confession will enable you to experience them.

The things we hear and think about will eventually find their way into our conversation. Guard what goes into your ears and eyes to keep your mind on the things of God.

"Bow down thine ear, and hear the words of the wise, and apply thine heart unto my knowledge. For it is a pleasant thing if thou keep them within thee; they shall withal be fitted in thy lips. That thy trust may be in the Lord, I have made known to thee this day, even to thee, Have not I written to thee excellent things in counsels and knowledge, That I might make thee know the certainty of the words of truth to them that send unto thee" (Proverbs 22:17-21).

CALL THINGS
THAT ARE NOT AS THOUGH THEY WERE

Abraham is known as the father of our faith. He was required to believe God's Word and obey when all the natural circumstances opposed it. A verse in the book of Romans about Abraham gives us insight into the God-kind of faith.

"As it is written, I have made thee a father of many nations, before him whom he believed, even God, who quickeneth the dead, and calleth those things which be not as though they were" (Romans 4:17).

God talks about things that are not as if they were, that is, the things that have not become visible to the physical senses, but God sees them by faith. God can do this because He has faith in His own Word. He is confident that His Word will be accomplished.

God used His Word to create the world. (Hebrews 11:3) Notice how many times the phrase "And God said" appears in Genesis One. God is a God of faith. **God believes, speaks, and things happen.**

We have been given God's Word to act in faith as He did. His Word is full of creative power and it is for us now. Think about it. God has washed us with the blood of His Son, given us His life and nature, translated us into His Kingdom, lifted us into heavenly places, given us all things, filled us with His Spirit, and given us His Word. Should there be any reason we could not follow and imitate Jesus? What does "Christian" mean after all?

"For the word of God is quick, and powerful, and sharper than any twoedged sword, piercing even to the dividing asunder of soul and spirit, and of the joints and marrow, and is a discerner of the thoughts and intents of the heart" (Hebrews 4:12).

After we hear the Word, we believe, pray and receive accordingly. The Word will become manifested in our lives as we then begin to speak it by faith. God hastens to perform His Word. (Jeremiah 1:12.) This divine truth should encourage us to "hold fast the profession of our faith without wavering; (for he is faithful that promised)" (Hebrews 10:23). **The continual believing and confessing of God's Word releases the power of faith.**

God creates the fruit of the lips. (Isaiah 57:19.) The children of Israel discovered this truth at the time of their rebellion in the wilderness. Their unbelief caused them to reject God's Word which had promised rich blessings in the land of Canaan. They said, ". . . would God we had died in this wilderness" (Numbers 14:2).

God gave them their request as He said unto them, "As truly as I live, saith the Lord, as ye have spoken in mine ears, so will I do to you: Your carcases shall fall in this wilderness" (Numbers 14:28-29). This one story should be enough to convince anyone that words are important to God.

LESSON OF THE FIG TREE

Jesus operated every day of His ministry in these principles of faith. Each one of these parts of faith had been perfected to the point that Jesus could speak and instantly there would be results.

One of the most unusual accounts in the Bible about Jesus concerns faith confession and a fig tree.

"And on the morrow, when they were come from Bethany, he was hungry: And seeing a fig tree afar off having leaves, he came, if haply he might find any thing thereon: and when he came to it, he found nothing but leaves; for the time of figs was not yet. And Jesus answered and said unto it, No man eat fruit of thee hereafter for ever. And his disciples heard it . . . And in the morning, as they passed by, they saw the fig tree dried up from the roots. And Peter calling to remembrance saith unto him, Master, behold, the fig tree which thou cursedst is withered away" (Mark 11:12-14, 20-21).

Jesus spoke directly to the tree and His words became reality. The power of faith released out of His mouth changed the natural circumstances. Jesus used this same power to deliver a boy with a dumb spirit. Jesus ". . . rebuked the foul spirit, saying unto him, Thou dumb and deaf spirit, I charge thee, come out of him, and enter no more into him" (Mark 9:25). Jesus believed that what He said would come to pass, and the boy was delivered.

Over and over again, Jesus used His faith to help people. He spoke to the leper, ". . . be thou clean. And as soon as he had spoken, immediately the leprosy departed from him and he was cleansed" (Mark 1:41-42).

Jesus spoke to the paralytic, "Arise, and take up thy bed, and go thy way into thine house. And immediately he arose, took up the bed, and went forth before them all" (Mark 2:11-12).

Jesus used His faith to stop the destructive forces of a storm on the sea. "And he arose, and rebuked the wind, and said unto the sea, Peace, be still. And the wind ceased, and there was a great calm" (Mark 4:39).

Even death was loosed from a little girl by the power of Jesus' words. "Damsel, I say unto thee, arise. And straightway the damsel arose, and walked" (Mark 5:41).

How could Jesus do these things? Was it because He was God's Son? You are now one of the sons of God. (Galatians 4:6.) Was it because God gave Jesus a special commission to do these things? You have the same commission. (Mark 16:15-18, John 14:12.) Was it because Jesus had a special anointing of the Holy Spirit? You have the command to receive a special anointing too. (Acts 1:4,8; Luke 24:49.) Jesus is our example, and we are to follow in His steps ministering to those in need.

Let's go back to the fig tree. After Peter brought Jesus' attention to the withered tree, Jesus explained to His disciples the principle of faith confession.

"And Jesus answering said unto them, Have faith in God. For verily I say unto you, That whosoever shall say unto this mountain, Be thou removed, and be thou cast into the sea; and shall not doubt in his heart, but shall believe that those things which he saith shall come to pass; he shall have whatsoever he saith. Therefore I say unto you, What things soever ye desire, when ye pray, believe that ye receive them, and ye shall have them" (Mark 11:22-24).

Jesus intends for us to use the power of faith confession in every area of our lives. He said we are to live by every Word that comes from the mouth of God. (Matthew 4:4.) The Word further tells us, " . . . The just shall live by faith" (Romans 1:17). Jesus used His faith to heal, raise the dead, provide bread and fishes for thousands, stop storms, pay taxes and defeat the devil.

Jesus makes it plain that human beings who believe in Him can operate in faith **exactly as He did—even to the extent of moving mountains.** The reason more Christians are not experiencing the joys of victorious faith is they fail to **consistently** operate the principles of faith. The God-kind of faith is not developed overnight. It grows by continual hearing, believing, praying, receiving, confessing, meditating, praising, doing, hearing, believing, praying, receiving, confessing, meditating, praising, and doing the Word and so forth."

You can have what you say if you will believe and speak in accordance with God's will—His Word. God wants you and me to have more good things than we can even think of or desire. He is our heavenly Father and He loves His children. I am wonderfully blessed to be able to say, "God is my Father and Jesus is my Lord."

THE SWORD

"Above all, taking the shield of faith, wherewith ye shall be able to quench all the fiery darts of the wicked. And take the helmet of salvation, and the sword of the Spirit, which is the word of God".
(Ephesians 6:16-17).

Our shield and sword are connected. Faith comes by hearing God's Word. (Romans 10:17.) They go together. The Word builds our faith. Faith causes us to use the Word as a weapon. All of the armor listed in Ephesians 6:10-18 comes from God's Word and must be put on by faith.

The Word of God is an offensive weapon for the Christian. It is the Word on our lips that overcomes the powers of darkness. "And this is the victory that overcometh the world, even our faith" (I John 5:4). Faith in God's Word must be released out of our own mouth as a positive confession.

God has given us the Word to stand against the attacks of the devil. But until we resist him by speaking God's Word, he will not flee. Jesus proved the power of the spoken Word when He was tempted by satan in the wilderness. (Matthew 4:1-11.) Three times He said, "It is written," and quoted passages from the Law. Finally, the devil left Him, defeated by the Word of God.

In the book of Revelation, Jesus reveals to us that the saints will use the spoken Word to overcome the devil. "And they overcame him by the blood of the Lamb, and by the word of their testimony; and they loved not their lives unto the death" (Revelation 12:11).

Keep the Word in your heart, in your mind, and flowing out of your mouth. You will enjoy the blessings of abundant life and be able to share these blessings with others.

WATCH YOUR MOUTH

"Let no corrupt communication proceed out of your mouth, but that which is good to the use of edifying, that it may minister grace unto the hearers" (Ephesians 4:29).

"Set a watch, O lord, before my mouth; keep the door of my lips" (Psalm 141:3).

"Let the words of my mouth, and the meditation of my heart, be acceptable in thy sight, O Lord, my strength, and my redeemer" (Psalm 19:14).

Start by confessing your faith NOW!

I am saved by grace through faith.

(Ephesians 2:8-10.)

I am a child of God and a joint-heir with Jesus Christ. (Romans 8:16-17.)

There is no condemnation in my life.

(Romans 8:1.)

The joy of the Lord is my strength.

(Nehemiah 8:10.)

The love of God is shed abroad in my heart.

(Romans 5:5.)

I have the power of the Holy Ghost to be a witness unto Jesus. (Acts 1:8.)

(If you desire additional verses to speak by faith, we have a pocket Scripture packet with over 75 verses in the first person that is available upon request.)

7

Meditation

"Meditate upon these things; give thyself wholly to them; that thy profiting may appear to all. Take heed unto thyself, and unto the doctrine; continue in them: for in doing this thou shalt both save thyself, and them that hear thee" (I Timothy 4:15-16).

Meditation of God's Word involves the spirit, soul, and body simultaneously. The Greek word "meletao" means to revolve in the mind or imagine. As we continually think about the truth of the Word, our mind will be purified, faith will come into our heart, and our tongue will be brought under control.

KEYS TO PROSPERITY AND SUCCESS

God gave Joshua three keys to prosperity and success. "This book of the law shall not depart out of thy mouth; but thou shalt meditate therein day and night that thou mayest observe to do according to all that is written therein: for then thou shalt make thy way prosperous, and then thou shalt have good success" (Joshua 1:8).

1. **Keep God's Word in your mouth.**

2. **Meditate upon God's Word day and night.**

3. **Do according to all of God's Word.**

What a joy to live by God's Word. His commandments are not grievous. (I John 5:3.) He has told us to delight ourselves in Him. (Psalm 37:4.) The

Word of God is spirit and life to us. (John 6:63.) He
feeds our spirit man with the bread of life. (John 6:51.)
As we meditate upon God's Word, we are eating the
flesh of the Son of man. (John 6:53-58.) This living
bread gives us eternal life.

The Hebrew word for meditate, "hagah," means to
murmur, ponder, imagine, mutter, speak, study, or
utter. As we meditate the Word, we are talking it
over to ourselves. We form the words with our lips,
think about them and say them slowly. Then phrase by
phrase and word by word, we repeat the process back-
wards and forwards. The truth begins to grow in our
mind and sink into our heart as we speak forth what
God is revealing to our understanding.

The psalmist gives us an even greater apprecia-
tion for meditation of God's Word.

*"Blessed is the man that walketh not in the
counsel of the ungodly, nor standeth in the way of
sinners, nor sitteth in the seat of the scornful. But his
delight is in the law of the Lord; and in his law doth
he meditate day and night. And he shall be like a tree
planted by the rivers of water, that bringeth forth his
fruit in his season; his leaf also shall not wither; and
whatsoever he doeth shall prosper"* (Psalm 1:1-3).

As we meditate, we are hiding God's Word in our
spirit. It is being fixed into our thought patterns. Our
lips are learning to speak the truth. We are being conformed to the image of Jesus Christ with the end
result of continuous prosperity and blessing in spirit,
soul, and body.

The man dedicated to meditating and obeying
God's Word will be flourishing when others are falling
by the wayside. Even in times of drought, his leaf will

remain green and he will continue to bear fruit. This is paralleled with a tree planted by the rivers of water. The roots go down deep, below the river bed, where there will be water even in times of difficulty. Our lives will bear love, joy, and peace even in times when others are depressed, confused and full of hatred.

ABIDING IN THE VINE

Jesus compared our relationship to Him with a branch's relationship to its vine. The believer can do nothing apart from Christ. But the believer who keeps a vital contact with Jesus can ask anything in prayer and it will be done.

"I am the vine, ye are the branches: He that abideth in me, and I in him, the same bringeth forth much fruit: for without me ye can do nothing. If a man abide not in me, he is cast forth as a branch, and is withered; and men gather them, and cast them into the fire, and they are burned. If ye abide in me, and my words abide in you, ye shall ask what ye will, and it shall be done unto you" (John 15:5-7).

During our meditation of the Word, we are seeking to ground and settle our faith. It is a time to remove all doubt and fix heart, soul, and body on the truth. Many times the Word will drop into our spirit and the overwhelming confidence of faith will come forth from within us. Up until this time we may have struggled for faith, but now we know that we know that we know—IT IS DONE.

"Let the word of Christ dwell in you richly in all wisdom" (Colossians 3:16). Revelation understanding and wisdom often come only after we meditate on what we have heard or read. It is the understanding and wisdom that show us how to apply God's knowledge in our lives.

CONTROLLING YOUR IMAGINATIONS

One of the major battlegrounds for faith is the imagination. Ideas, thoughts, and imaginations can work for or against you. Continual meditation of God's Word can give you victory in this area.

"For the weapons of our warfare are not carnal, but mighty through God to the pulling down of strong holds; Casting down imaginations, and every high thing that exalteth itself against the knowledge of God, and bringing into captivity every thought to the obedience of Christ" (II Corinthians 10:4-6).

As you fix the Word in your mind, speak it over to yourself, and revolve it in your heart, you will be able to gain total control of your thought life. It does not happen overnight because mind renewal is a process. It takes time to learn and meditate on each area of God's Word. You will conquer each area by the power of God just as Joshua led Israel to take the promised land. It will take time to study the Word and use your faith to claim each promise, but you have the confidence that the truth will set you totally free.

"That ye put off concerning the former conversation the old man, which is corrupt according to the deceitful lusts; And be renewed in the spirit of your mind; And that ye put on the new man, which after God is created in righteousness and true holiness" (Ephesians 4:22-24).

Do not be discouraged if you momentarily lapse back into anger or lust. Ask your Father to forgive your sin and cleanse you from all unrighteousness. (I John 1:9.) Start over again by reviewing the promises. **Take spiritual revenge on your disobedience.** That is, spend extra time hearing, believing, praying, receiving, confessing, meditating, praising and acting on the area of God's Word in which you failed. God will put you over. His ability, power, strength, and might have not changed one bit.

Do not ever give up the fight of faith. Although you may come to the point that you stop trying to do it all yourself, you are not giving up. Just let God do the part He has promised to do. Your part is faith. **Play until you win.** Remember, you are on the winning team. Jesus has already defeated satan. (Matthew 28:18.) He gave us the victory. (Mark 16:17-18, II Corinthians 2:14.) And in the final outcome, all opposition will be put away forever. (Revelation 20:10.)

LOOKING UNTO JESUS

"Wherefore seeing we also are compassed about with so great a cloud of witnesses, let us lay aside every weight, and the sin which doth so easily beset us, and let us run with patience the race that is set before us, Looking unto Jesus the author and finisher of our faith; who for the joy that was set before him endured the cross, despising the shame, and is set down at the right hand of the throne of God" (Hebrews 12:1-2).

Never forget that our faith is in Jesus, JESUS, **JESUS.** It is His life, His power, His blessings, His truth, His strength. He is our Savior, Lord, High Priest, and King. As we meditate on the Word, we can visualize Jesus seated at the right hand of God and at the same time know He is living in us by His Spirit and Word. He is the One who mediates the promises of the new covenant and guarantees their fulfillment. (Hebrews 8:6; 7:22.)

BLESSINGS OF MEDITATION ON GOD'S WORD

"My son, attend to my words; incline thine ear unto my sayings, Let them not depart from thine eyes; keep them in the midst of thine heart. For they are life unto those that find them, and health to all their flesh. Keep thy heart with all diligence; for out of it are the issues of life"

(Proverbs 4:20-23).

Meditation is like eating God's Word. As we chew on it and the food is digested, we receive strength and health for our spirit, soul, body.

"My son, keep thy father's commandment, and forsake not the law of thy mother; Bind them continually upon thine heart and tie them about thy neck. When thou goest, it shall lead thee; when thou sleepest it shall keep thee; and when thou awakest, it shall talk with thee. For the commandment is a lamp; and the law is light; and reproofs of instruction are the way of life"

(Proverbs 6:20-23).

Meditation will cause you to dream about the Word and have it come to your mind the first thing in the morning. Wouldn't that be great! Imagine waking up thinking, "This is the day the Lord hath made, I will rejoice and be glad in it." What a change from, "OOOHHH, another day, UUUUUUHHHHHHHH."

The Word will also speak to you through the day to guide you in the straight and narrow way. People have wondered how in the world they could ever live by the Sermon on The Mount. But the moment Jesus comes inside you, you have the potential to live by God's Word. Jesus is the only One who will ever be able to live the LIFE, and praise God, He is living in us. We **can** and **will** let Him live through us.

WHEN TO MEDITATE

All the time! While you will want to set aside a time for quiet time alone, you can meditate on God's Word anywhere, at anytime. Even while you are working at home, at school, or in the office, you can dwell on such good thoughts as, "I can do all things through Christ who strengthens me. I am more than a conqueror through Him who loved me. All things are working together for good in my life. I have the mind of Christ." (Philippians 4:13; Romans 8:37, 28; I Corinthians 2:16.)

Actually, meditation of God's Word should be a way of life for the Christian. Jesus has promised never to leave or forsake us. (Hebrews 13:5.) Why should we ignore Him? We can acknowledge His presence continually by meditating on His Word.

. "Thou wilt keep him in perfect peace, whose mind is stayed on thee: because he trusteth in thee" (Isaiah 26:3).

FAITH GROWS

In Jesus' parable of the sower sowing the Word, the hundredfold producers are those who "hear the word, and receive it, and bring forth fruit" (Mark 4:20). From the time the Word is first sown until it produces one-hundredfold, there must be a lot of attention given to its care and nurture in our lives.

Giving ourselves to meditation on the Word is like watering, fertilizing, and weeding the field. The more time given to it, the greater the crop yield and the quicker the harvest. Growing faith is no accident. God will cause it to grow, but we must be diligent to do our part.

8

Praise

Great emphasis is being placed on the power of praise in Christian teaching today. God is tuning up our faith and this is a very important part.

Praise seems to be the thing that gets our faith off the ground. An airplane may taxi up and down the runway just below takeoff speed and never get into the air to go anywhere. Not until the speed is increased and the pilot pulls back on the controls will the plane lift off the runway.

Some struggle for hours trying to believe and confess the Word, but seemingly experience no results. Real faith is a rest in which the believer knows **at the outset** that God's Word will not fail. Although there is a fight of faith, it is God who fights for us as we maintain our confidence and faith in His ability. Praise and thanksgiving are two of the most important elements in this faith fight because they express true faith.

Praise incorporates all of the other parts of faith. It is a confident prayer. Praise rejoices over hearing the Word and believing its truth. There is joy because it believes it has received. Praise confidently confesses while meditating on God's power. Praise acts as if God's Word is true. Praise is an attitude or way of life that rejoices continually in every situation.

WITH THANKSGIVING

"Be careful for nothing; but in every thing by prayer and supplication with thanksgiving let your

requests be made known unto God. And the peace of God, which passeth all understanding, shall keep your hearts and minds through Christ Jesus. Finally, brethren, whatsoever things are true, whatsoever things are honest, whatsoever things are just, whatsoever things are pure, whatsoever things are lovely, whatsoever things are of good report; if there be any virtue, and if there be any praise, think on these things" (Philippians 4:6-8).

The moment we pray, we begin to give thanks for God's provision. In fact, all prayer should be with thanksgiving. There are many words that express the idea of praise. Thanksgiving accompanies praise and vice versa. Other words that express praise are: rejoice, joy, gladness, singing, worship, happy, cheer, and life. Although each of these words have different meanings, they can all be part of our faith praise.

"Continue in prayer, and watch in the same with thanksgiving" (Colossians 4:2). Prayer and thanksgiving go hand in hand. We do not have to see the answer before we give thanks. We have God's Word. It is more sure than heaven and earth. (Matthew 24:35.)

Here is a Biblical pattern for approaching God. Notice how the elements of praise and thanksgiving stand out.

"Make a joyful noise unto the Lord, all ye lands. Serve the Lord with gladness: come before his presence with singing. Know ye that the Lord he is God: it is he that hath made us, and not we ourselves; we are his people, and the sheep of his pasture. Enter into his gates with thanksgiving, and into his courts with praise: be thankful unto him, and bless his name. For the Lord is good; his mercy is everlasting; and his truth endureth to all generations" (Psalm 100).

Come before God with an attitude of rejoicing. He is your Father and He loves you. Faith in the integrity of God's Word will give you an attitude of praise and confidence as you come before Him in prayer. Without faith people sink into despair, doom and gloom. Long faces, frowns, and moodiness are not consistent with the God-kind of faith.

CONTINUAL PRAISE

"By him therefore let us offer the sacrifice of praise to God continually, that is, the fruit of our lips giving thanks to his name" (Hebrews 13:15).

We can praise God continually because He never changes. Situations, circumstances, governments, weather, people, and the earth may change, but God's Word is constant. "Jesus Christ the same yesterday, and today, and forever" (Hebrews 13:8).

By laying the foundation of our faith on the solid rock of God's Word, we can praise God even in the midst of the storm with its waves and wind. We know that God can change any circumstance or situation that is not according to His will. "Rejoice evermore. Pray without ceasing. In everything give thanks: for this is the will of God in Christ Jesus concerning you" (I Thessalonians 5:16-18).

Jesus told us we would have tribulation. He did not try to mislead us into thinking that the Christian life had no problems here on the earth. Yet at the same time, He assured us of victory over tribulations and afflictions. Jesus is our victory, our answer, our way, and our solution.

"These things I have spoken unto you, that in me ye might have peace. In the world ye shall have tribulation: but be of good cheer; I have overcome the world" (John 16:33). Every tribulation or difficulty is an opportunity to demonstrate the power of God. (II Corinthians 12:10.)

CHEER UP! Jesus has overcome the world, and Jesus lives in our hearts. Peace, peace, wonderful peace—it is ours in Jesus. And there is more besides. Joy is in the Kingdom too. "For the kingdom of God is not meat and drink but righteousness, peace, and joy in the Holy Ghost" (Romans 14:17).

The prophet Habakkuk heard from God concerning the idea of rejoicing in joy and praise in spite of outward circumstances. Take notice of the things he lists that would not steal his joy.

"*Although the fig tree shall not blossom, neither shall fruit be in the vines; the labour of the olive shall fail, and the fields shall yield no meat; the flock shall be cut off from the fold, and there shall be no herd in the stall: Yet I will rejoice in the Lord, I will joy in the God of my salvation*" (Habakkuk 3:17-18).

God will make a way when there is seemingly no way at all. Our God will supply our needs regardless of what is going on in the world. His supply does not go up and down with the stock market averages. **He is more than enough.** Glory to God! Rejoice! You are His child, His heir, His property—and He loves you. If He gave you Jesus would He withhold any good thing of lesser value? No, of course not. He has given us freely all things. (Romans 8:32.)

OPENING PRISON DOORS

Paul and Silas were thrown into the inner prison at Philippi. They had been severely beaten, and now their feet were fast in the stocks. (Acts 16:23-24.)

"And at midnight Paul and Silas prayed and sang praises unto God: and the prisoners heard them. And suddenly there was a great earthquake, so that the foundations of the prison were shaken: and immediately all the doors were opened, and every one's bands were loosed" (Acts 16:25-26).

Praise **by faith** breaks the chains and fetters. Notice the horrible circumstances and reasons that should have kept them from praising God. But to Paul and Silas, God had not changed just because they were temporarily bound in prison and hurting in their body. They made an effort to ignore their flesh and release the Spirit of God within them.

Praise may require sacrificing the natural inclinations when there is no feeling or visible answer. Yet God is still there. He is worthy of our praise. We praise Him and thank Him because we love Him. Genuine love is not based on feelings or emotions but rather upon a quality choice that GIVES FIRST, regardless of the circumstances.

"Let the saints be joyful in glory: let them sing aloud upon their beds. Let the high praises of God be in their mouth, and a two edged sword in their hand" (Psalm 149:5-6).

With the Word in our mouth and praise on our lips we can bind the power of satan and loose the power of God. (Psalm 149:7-9, Matthew 18:18.) **Praise confession of the Word is a mighty sword** that will shake the very gates of hell. People will be freed, healed and delivered as we use this awesome weapon God has given us.

PRAISE IN THE FACE OF THE ENEMY

At the time Jehoshaphat was King of Judah, the armies of Moab, Ammon and Mt. Seir came against God's people to do battle. (II Chronicles 20.) As the King called the people to prayer and fasting, the Spirit spoke through Jahaziel, "Thus saith the Lord unto you, Be not afraid nor dismayed by reason of this great multitude; for the battle is not yours, but God's. Ye shall not need to fight in this battle: set yourselves, stand ye still, and see the salvation of the Lord with you, O Judah and Jerusalem: fear not, nor be dismayed; tomorrow go out against them: for the Lord will be with you" (Verses 15,17).

When the problem arose, the King and people knew **who** to go to. They believed in God's ability to deliver them for they had heard how He delivered the children of Israel from the Egyptians. Now, it was time to pray and receive God's Word for their need. After the Lord spoke to them, they praised and worshiped God.

The next day Jehoshaphat stood before the people and positively confessed his faith in God's Word. "Believe in the Lord your God, so shall ye be established; believe his prophets, so shall ye prosper" (Verse 20). The amazing thing about this victory was the plan that God gave to Judah. **They were to use the power of singing and praise to defeat the enemy.**

"And when he had consulted with the people, he appointed singers unto the Lord, and that should praise the beauty of holiness, as they went out before the army, and to say, Praise the Lord; for his mercy

endureth for ever. And when they began to sing and to praise, the Lord set ambushments against the children of Ammon, Moab, and mount Seir, which were come against Judah; and they were smitten" (Verses 21,22).

This miracle of victory through praise by faith is consistent with Psalm 149 and Acts 16. The praise, rejoicing and singing preceeds the physical manifestation of God fulfilling His Word.

FULL JOY

"And the angel said unto them, Fear not: for, behold, I bring you good tidings of great joy, which shall be to all people. For unto you is born this day in the city of David a Saviour, which is Christ the Lord" (Luke 2:10-11).

The birth of Jesus into the world brought great joy; the birth of Christ into our hearts should bring even greater joy. This, to me, is the reason we can rejoice and praise God. We know that our names are written in heaven the moment we make Jesus our Lord, and this is what Jesus said to rejoice over. (Luke 10:20.)

"Therefore the redeemed of the Lord shall return, and come with singing unto Zion; and everlasting joy shall be upon their head: they shall obtain gladness and joy; and sorrow and mourning shall flee away" (Isaiah 51:11). The life of singing and rejoicing, with joy and gladness, is actually what God planned for His children.

Jesus came to bring good news of healing and liberty; "To appoint unto them that mourn in Zion, to give unto them beauty for ashes, the oil of joy for mourning, the garment of praise for the spirit of heaviness; that they might be called trees of righteousness, the planting of the Lord, that he might be glorified" (Isaiah 61:3).

Praise is the acceptable garment for the believer. **So keep it on all the time.** You have been given the name that commands attention in heaven and earth. "And in that day ye shall ask me nothing. Verily, verily, I say unto you, Whatsoever ye shall ask the Father in my name, he will give it to you. Hitherto have ye asked nothing in my name: ask, and ye shall receive, that your joy may be full" (John 16:23-24).

Full joy comes when you pray and know you receive because you have asked in the name of Jesus. This is your privilege: to enjoy your salvation continually. Rejoice! Praise God!

9

Do The Word . . .
Obey, Keep, Act, Fulfill

Although we have given eight different parts of faith, Jesus spoke of only two in building our lives upon the rock: Hear it and do it. **Simple obedience to God's Word is what faith is all about.**

"Therefore whosoever heareth these sayings of mine, and doeth them, I will liken him unto a wise man, which built his house upon a rock: and the rain descended, and the floods came, and the winds blew, and beat upon that house; and it fell not: for it was founded upon a rock. And every one that heareth these sayings of mine, and doeth them not, shall be likened unto a foolish man, which built his house upon the sand: And the rain descended, and the floods came, and the winds blew, and beat upon that house; and it fell: and great was the fall of it" (Matthew 7:24-27).

The wise man is both a **hearer** and a **doer.** Throughout the Bible there are wonderful accounts of men and women receiving great blessings because they **did** what God told them.

Noah started building an ark when there was no flood. The natural mind will often rebel against obeying God's Word because it seems to be nonsense, but Noah had God's Word. "The natural man receiveth not the things of the Spirit of God: for they are foolishness unto him" (I Corinthians 2:14).

Abraham started up the mountain to sacrifice his only son in simple obedience to God's command. He knew that Isaac was the one through whom God would bless all the nations, yet he climbed upward with the full intention of carrying out God's instructions.

As Peter leaned over the edge of the boat, he heard Jesus speak one powerful word, "COME." (Matthew 14:29.) Faith acted, and Peter also walked on the water. It was the natural circumstances that caused him to sink: his senses and feelings told him he could not walk on the sea. Doubt, disguised as reason, won the battle over faith.

The accounts of Noah, Abraham, and Peter show the importance of utilizing all the parts of faith. The effects of time, circumstance, and public opinion can be disastrous to faith if the Word has not been fully established by hearing, believing, praying, receiving, confessing, meditating, praising, and doing.

GO AND WASH IN JORDAN

The principle of doing according to God's Word in order to receive miracles is not new. Naaman, the Syrian, had leprosy and needed a miracle of healing in his life. He heard of the prophet Elisha in Israel and went to his house for healing. What a surprise he got! Elisha would not even see him personally, but sent a servant instead to give him the formula for healing.

"So Naaman came with his horses and with his chariot, and stood at the door of the house of Elisha. And Elisha sent a messenger unto him, saying, Go and wash in Jordan seven times, and thy flesh shall come again to thee, and thou shalt be clean. but Naaman was wroth and went away, and said, Behold, I thought, He will surely come out to me, and stand,

*and call on the name of the Lord his God, and strike
his hand over the place, and recover the leper. Are not
Abana and Pharpar, rivers of Damascus, better than
all the waters of Israel? May I not wash in them, and
be clean? So he turned and went away in a rage"*
(II Kings 5:8-12).

It just did not make good sense to Naaman.
Elisha's idea just had no reason about it, and you can
imagine what Naaman was thinking. The River Jordan
was so dirty compared to the beautiful rivers of
Damascus. And why couldn't Elisha just wave his hand
over me and remove the leprosy? Truly God has
chosen "the foolish things of the world to confound
the wise" (I Corinthians 1:27).

There is a great lesson to learn from the story of
Naaman's healing. God could have used Elisha to speak
a word, touch him, pray for him, or merely wave his
hand to heal him; but instead God instructed Elisha to
tell Naaman to act out his faith. He has to do something with his own body of flesh before he could
receive his healing. Naaman's pride rejected God's
command and only after his servant encouraged him
did he respond to the instructions.

*"And his servant came near, and spake unto him,
and said, My father, if the prophet had bid thee do
some great thing, wouldest thou not have done it? how
much rather then, when he saith to thee, Wash, and
be clean? Then went he down, and dipped himself
seven times in Jordan, according to the saying of the
man of God: and his flesh came again like unto the
flesh of a little child, and he was clean"* (II Kings
5:13-14).

Simple obedience brought the healing. God often
gives instructions for receiving miracles that seem

strange from man's limited viewpoint. The important thing is to obey and let God take care of the rest.

SNAKE ON A POLE

When the children of Israel sinned and began to be bitten by fiery serpents, God gave Moses the solution. He was to make a serpent out of brass and lift it up on a pole. God said he would heal the people as they looked at the brazen serpent. (Numbers 21:4-9.) It may have seemed ridiculous at the time, but it worked. Now, we know it was a type of Calvary that tells us we can look on Jesus for healing. (John 3:14-17.)

MARCH AROUND AND KEEP YOUR MOUTH SHUT

One of the most unusual victories that Israel won in the conquest of Canaan was at Jericho. Joshua received the directions from God on how to take the city. To the natural mind, God's battle plans would have seemed foolish. Yet God had His signals straight, and Joshua obeyed the Word of the Lord.

God commanded the priests to carry the ark around the city six days and on the seventh day go around seven times and then blow their trumpets. The men of war were to follow them **silently** the first six days but on the seventh day as the trumpets sounded they were to shout with a great shout.

The people obeyed God's command and exactly as they were told, the walls fell down flat. God fulfilled His Word to them as they obeyed His commandments. This should encourage us to do what God has told us even if it seems foolish or unimportant. God has always blessed the obedient.

A DOER

"But be ye doers of the word, and not hearers only, deceiving your own selves. For if any be a hearer of the word, and not a doer, he is like unto a man beholding his natural face in a glass: For he beholdeth himself, and goeth his way, and straightway forgetteth what manner of man he was. But whoso looketh into the perfect law of liberty, and continueth therein, he being not a forgetful hearer, but a doer of the word, this man shall be blessed in his deed" (James 1:22-25).

Unless we **do the Word** we can deceive ourselves into thinking that we are pleasing God when we are not. It is doing those things that are pleasing in God's sight that gives us confidence before God. (I John 3:21-22.) Many hear the Word, believe the Word, and speak the Word, but only the **doers** are blessed by God. This gives us a clear understanding of why we must operate all the parts of faith.

God's Word is called the "perfect law of liberty." His Word is pure, refined, inspired—perfect. The Word gives us the truth, and it is this truth that sets us free. By continuing in the Word (hearing, reading, studying, speaking, memorizing, meditating and doing) we will be set totally free in our lives—spirit, soul, and body.

Just as a person looks in the mirror to "check himself," so we look into God's Word to check our new creation. As Christians we have been recreated for the purpose of being conformed to the image of Christ. The continual observance of this new nature as revealed in God's Word will establish in our minds the type of person God has made us in our spirit. Once we know the truth, we will act accordingly and submit our body to the Word of God.

LOVE PERFECTED

"But whoso keepeth his word, in him verily is the love of God perfected: hereby know we that we are in him" (I John 2:5).

Feelings and circumstances should have nothing to do with DOING THE WORD. There will be times you may feel hatred or bitterness, yet God's Word says "Love your enemies" (Matthew 5:44). Just tell yourself, "You are going to love and you will not hate." Some may ask how can I do that when I don't feel it in my heart? Think about the millions of Americans who get up and go to work on Monday morning when they don't even feel like it at all. How do they do it? They have to; it's part of their job. So it is with us. **We do the Word** because we know it pleases the Father. Plus, we receive the benefits of the fulfillment of His promises. **The doers of the Word are the receivers of the blessings.**

Our love takes on a consistency as we do the Word. We love in spite of the people, and their attitude toward us. Jesus loved this way. On the cross He said, "Father forgive them; for they know not what they do" (Luke 23:34). His love was perfected. In the most difficult and trying circumstances, only love came forth. **He was a doer of the Word.**

DOERS ARE FAMILY MEMBERS

One day as Jesus preached to the multitudes, His family came calling on Him. The crowd told Him that His mother and brethren were trying to get to Him. As Jesus looked around at the people, He uttered a remarkable statement: "Behold my mother and my brethren! For whosoever shall do the will of God, the

same is my brother, and my sister, and mother"
(Mark 3:34-35).

The family of God is made up of those who do His
will. Salvation requires doing the Word. We are saved
by grace through faith. (Ephesians 2:8.) Yet faith
without works is dead. (James 2:26.) "Ye see then how
that by works a man is justified, and not by faith
only" (James 2:24).

Doing the Word is simply acting in correspon-
dence with your believing and confessing. This
involves all three parts of man—spirit, soul, and body.
He that does the will of God abides forever. (I John
2:17.) "Ye know that every one that doeth
righteousness is born of him" (I John 2:29).

GET YOUR FEET WET FIRST

Sometimes we may believe, pray, receive, confess,
and praise God for some provision but never see the
results until we act on it. Such was the case when the
children of Israel entered the promised land after forty
years in the desert.

The Lord had spoken to Joshua concerning the
conquest of Canaan. The entire land was promised to
Israel if they would just do as God commanded. The
first test of faith came in crossing the swollen waters
of the Jordan River. It may seem small, but it was a
pattern for all future believers who would dare to
possess the land of promise.

Joshua gave a command for the ark of the covenant to pass over the Jordan first. The priests were to
carry the ark towards the river in confidence that God
would divide the water as soon as the soles of their
feet touched it. They did as God commanded, and the

waters parted allowing Israel to pass over on dry ground.

Step out on God's Word. Your faith will make a way for others to pass over onto the victory side too. Remember, Peter did not know the thrill of standing on water until he got out of the boat.

The loaves and fishes did not multiply until the disciples began to distribute them by faith.

The blind man was healed when he washed in the pool of Siloam.

The paralytic was healed because his friends tore up a roof and lowered him before Jesus.

Just read the New Testament again, and mark the places where people were required to act on their faith to receive miracles in their lives. God wants us to do something with our faith. Sometimes it will come directly from the Bible as we read it or hear it. At other times as we pray, the Spirit will tell us what to do to release our faith. The Spirit and the Word will always minister together if we are open to listen. Learn to know the voice of God. Do what He says; you will be blessed.

"To obey is better than sacrifice" (I Samuel 15:22).

10

Necessary Additives

There are many optional additives on the market today which claim to make the car engine run smoother, quieter, longer, get better gas mileage, and reduce wear on parts. Cars themselves have many luxury options which make riding much more pleasant and enjoyable. These additions and options may not be absolutely necessary, but they can be very helpful.

However, some parts of the car are just plain necessary, without them there would be no use for the engine. Such items as gasoline, oil, starter, and battery are required on standard V-8 engines. The car itself must have brakes, gears, tires, accelerator, and a steering wheel. When we think of a car, we naturally include these necessary parts in our thinking.

In this book we have talked primarily about the **parts** of faith. There is so much more that could be said about the total Christain life, yet we do want to point out these necessary elements which the Word of God tells us to add to our faith. Without them, we would never accomplish what God has planned for us.

"And beside this, giving all diligence, add to your faith virtue; and to virtue knowledge; and to knowledge temperance; and to temperance patience; and to patience godliness; and to godliness brotherly kindness; and to brotherly kindness charity. For if these things be in you, and abound, they make you that ye shall neither be barren nor unfruitful in the knowledge of our Lord Jesus Christ" (II Peter 1:5-8).

VIRTUE

Virtue is excellence of moral character. Integrity, purity, and wholesomeness are words that help us understand virtue. We must undergird our faith with refined character and virtue if we intend to finish the course and win the fight of faith.

People may be amazed, thrilled, and challenged by great faith, but they will honor and respect virtue. In fact, virtue will protect faith from developing pride, greed, and many other vices that would eventually nullify it. People will be drawn to you because they see faith that is tempered with humility, honesty, integrity, fairness, simplicity, and gracefulness.

One friend shared how God dealt with him in the area of virtue. As a young minister he had a great desire to see mighty miracles, signs, and wonders in his services. As he began to pray, "Lord, give me power," he said he heard the Spirit of the Lord say, "Purity." Then he related that everytime he asked the Lord for miracles, God would deal with him about motives.

My friend related that the power and miracles did come, but only after some important issues had been settled in his heart. He had to determine the purpose of miracles and purify his motives for desiring them. Most of all, he had to settle the issue of who was going to get the glory.

God definitely wants to use you in ministering His power to a needy world; yet He loves you so much, He wants to keep you from pride, selfishness, and greed. **Add virtue to your faith,** and it will run purer and last longer.

KNOWLEDGE

Adding knowledge is the acquiring of spiritual truth. Learning the Word to know God's ways gives balance to faith. The quest for spiritual knowledge causes us to search all of God's Word to discover the whole counsel of God.

The suggestion has been made by several people to read through the entire Bible each year. This panoramic view of the plan of redemption gives a greater depth to our faith. As we call to remembrance the accounts of Abraham, Isaac, Jacob, Moses, Joshua, David, Peter, and Paul, our understanding of faith expands enormously. The central focus of our faith is on Jesus, so spend time in the New Testament—see yourself in Christ.

Knowledge can be added to our faith by studying topics in the Word. My heart thrilled as I began to see the correlation between God's love and Jesus' ministry of abundant life during His earth walk. Likewise, faith for healing by anointing with oil is strengthened when we understand the substitutionary sacrifice of Jesus Christ as the Lamb of God.

Personally, I have found the best approach to adding knowledge is starting and ending with Jesus. To explain, if you are going to study the gifts of the Spirit, start and end by seeing Jesus as the giver of the gifts. The same goes with healing, deliverance, power or prosperity; because Jesus is the author and finisher of our faith. (Hebrews 12:1-2.) Through the forgiveness of sins you have become an heir of God and joint-heir of Jesus Christ. (Romans 8:17.) There is so much wealth in our inheritance in Christ that we will be continuously learning of its benefits.

Continue to learn. Never say you have finally arrived. We are always getting there—daily. Pray "That the God of our Lord Jesus Christ, the Father of glory, may give unto you the spirit of wisdom and revelation in the knowledge of him" (Ephesians 1:17).

TEMPERANCE

The implication of the word temperance in this list of faith additives is that of properly using the knowledge acquired. Another word for temperance that gives light to our understanding is self-control. It is not just the hearers of the Word that are blessed, but rather those who **hear** and **do**.

Doing the Word requires self-control. Even though a person may know the Word, he will not be a consistent doer until his body and mind have been brought under control. Temperance then, means allowing the Word you know to rule your heart, soul, and body.

One day as I visited with a friend, we began to talk about our desire for more knowledge of the Word. Then he stopped and said, "If I could only live by what I already know, I would be doing great." For some, the quest for knowledge of new things may be an escape from facing the reality of submitting mind and body to do the Word. Let this be your prayer, "Father, I want to know your Word in order to do it."

Most often we think of temperance as moderation. This is avoidance of indulgence, excess, or extravagance in passions and appetites. Walking in the Spirit is God's remedy for overcoming the flesh, and it is a positive rather than a negative approach.

Before we can have a consistently strong faith, we must have a consistently strong spirit. Therefore, the mind must be renewed until it is casting down every evil imagination "that exalts itself against the knowledge of God and bringing into captivity every thought to the obedience of Christ" (II Corinthians 10:5). The body of flesh with its carnal desires must be reckoned dead and put to death by the spirit, the Word, and the blood. As the Word, the spirit, and the blood control and cleanse the mind and body, temperance is the natural result.

PATIENCE

Patience is more than just hanging on and waiting for something to happen. It is a force that comes forth from the heart and mind that causes things to happen through faith. Patience includes consistency, singleness of purpose, determination, endurance, and steadfastness.

The moment we see the possibilities of living by faith, our heart leaps for joy. Now there is hope to be all our Father wants us to be and enjoy all He has planned for us. But as we start taking God at His Word, we learn that everything does not happen instantly. Here is where we add the force of patience to our faith. There will no doubt be a battle in our lives to hold onto the new territory we have claimed by faith. Settle it beforehand; purpose in your heart, and determine that you will not be denied that which God has promised.

"Cast not away therefore your confidence, which hath great recompence of reward. For ye have need of patience, that, after ye have done the will of God, ye might receive the promise" (Hebrews 10:35-36).

Contrary to the world's idea of patience, the Word of God says that patience is added to faith to cause the

Word to be manifested in full possession. In other words, we do not let go of our faith if for some reason there is no visible change in circumstances. Instead of just HANGING ON we TURN IT ON, and apply the force of patience. That is, we continually acknowledge the Word and praise God for performing it in us. There is no wavering, rationalizing, or apologizing within our hearts; but rather a steadfast, persistent stand upon the eternal Word of God.

"And we desire that every one of you do shew the same diligence to the full assurance of hope unto the end: That ye be not slothful, but followers of them who through faith and patience inherit the promises" (Hebrews 6:11-12).

Notice that it takes both **faith** and **patience** to inherit God's promises. One of our close friends, Mr. Francis Weaver, shared with us his battle with cancer symptoms and how faith with patience in God's Word brought victory. Early in his Christian life he and his wife decided to live by God's Word. They faithfully claimed the promises for healing and received great miracles. One day Francis noticed a soreness in his chest. As he examined it he discovered a small growth. Recalling God's Word, he began to claim the promises of healing. The growth got bigger, and the pain got more intense. During the two years of this faith battle, Mr. Weaver faced many thoughts, feelings, and temptations that tried to come against him and shake him from his confession of faith. It was the force of patience—relentless, steadfast, unwavering—that gave him the strength to hold his faith. Finally, one day it was gone. Glory Hallelujah!

We can shout after the battle is over and won, but Jesus has called us to rejoice **in the midst** of tribulations, trials, and testings for He has overcome the world. (John 16:33.)

Never forget—JESUS WON, HE WINS, AND HE SHALL WIN!

GODLINESS

Godliness develops as we seek to please God. The godly person has heart, mind and will set on pleasing the Father. "If ye then be risen with Christ, seek those things which are above, where Christ sitteth on the right hand of God. Set your affection on things above, not on things on the earth" (Colossians 3:1-2). The end result of this continual seeking of the Father's pleasure is an attitude that is God-ward.

The need for godliness in the faith walk is paramount. The force of faith is powerful to meet the needs of many people if it is used wisely. It is not a power to be grasped selfishly, but rather to be cherished as a gift from the Father. Faith is to be used to fulfill His plans and purposes. Don't worry; He has your best interest at heart.

A young girl may learn just how to ask her daddy for a gift in order to get it. Daddy is pleased that she has asked and grants that which he is willing and able to give. But at the same time he looks forward to the day his girl will begin to ask, "Daddy, what can I do for you today?" She will have no problem getting the things she needs, but more importantly she will bring great joy to her father.

Godliness then, is that change of heart that causes our interests to turn from pleasing self to pleasing the One that loved us before the world began. We find our joy in giving Him joy. We become Father-pleasers,

intently seeking first His Kingdom. You will become
like the One you admire and desire to please the most.
You will begin to take on outwardly, His nature, His
attitudes, and His character.

Our Father has not left us in the dark as to how
to please Him. His Word reveals His plans, purposes
and desires for us as individuals and as the Church
body. His Word is His will. The two cannot be
separated for God's Word cannot fail. "Wherein he
hath abounded toward us in all wisdom and prudence;
Having made known unto us the mystery of his will
according to his good pleasure which he hath purposed
in himself" (Ephesians 1:8-9). If we keep His Word,
we can "walk worthy of the Lord unto all pleasing"
(Colossians 1:10).

Jesus said, "he that hath seen me hath seen the
Father" (John 14:9). Yet He also said, "I seek not
mine own will, but the will of the Father which hath
sent me" (John 5:30). Because He was a Father-
pleaser, the world could see the Father in Him. We
too will show the world the Father as we seek to
please Him. His life will be manifested in us that He
may be glorified.

You may wonder how you could ever be godly.
The enemy tries to keep Christians from developing
godliness through imaginations of false humility. The
thought that weakness and failure are signs of
meekness has kept many Christians from pressing into
the position of a Father-pleaser. It is an easy out just
to say "not everyone is a mountain mover." Read Mark
11:23 again. **Those who move mountains by faith are**
not the super-Christians, not the seminary graduates,
not the 40-year Christians, but **whosoever will.** Let's
face this issue squarely: the only ones who do not

move the mountains in their lives are those who **will not obey** what Jesus said. This could be because of lack of knowledge, doubt, or unbelief.

Whatever God has called us to do, to be, or to say, can be accomplished. Our Father has already supplied whatever it takes to get the job done. He never would have given us His Word if it could not be fulfilled in us. "According as his divine power hath given unto us all things that pertain unto life and godliness, through the knowledge of him that hath called us to glory and virtue" (II Peter 1:3).

The moment you receive Jesus, you have the power within you to live in godliness. "For it is God which worketh in you both to will and to do of his good pleasure" (Philippians 2:13). Rest in faith that God is doing and will do His good pleasure in your life. "For we are his workmanship" (Ephesians 2:10). Even godliness comes by faith. You have heard the Word. Faith should go into operation. You can please the Father and be transformed into His likeness. Your life will reflect godliness.

BROTHERLY KINDNESS

Showing kindness to a brother is really showing it to Christ. "Inasmuch as ye have done it unto one of the least of these my brethren, ye have done it unto me" (Matthew 25:40). This changes our whole perspective on kindness. It is not a matter of doing a good deed every day (which is not a bad idea) but rather a lifestyle of seeking to please Jesus by blessing His people.

Brotherly kindness prevents us from turning inward in our faith. As we see who we are in Christ, we should see who our brothers are in Christ. Jesus taught His disciples to pray "Our Father." (Matthew 6:9.) Although we should never minimize the importance of a personal relationship, we should also see that it is a family relationship too. We may have brothers and sisters who are younger, weaker, and different in their views on the Word. One good way to bring the family into a unity of the faith is through demonstrating brotherly kindness rather than brotherly arguments.

The Father desires that our love for others would be the most important thing in our lives next to loving Him. (Matthew 22:37-39.) In fact, He says that loving others is very similar to loving Him especially in the case of loving brothers in Christ.

Jesus said, "By this shall all men know that ye are my disciples, if ye have love one to another" (John 13:35). People see and understand acts of love and kindness. There is no mistaking this genuine fruit because folks love to eat it. Unselfish acts of brotherly kindness make family living a joy.

The hardness of the world is broken in a flash by an act of brotherly kindness. The light of Christ was so bright that the world could not even comprehend it. (John 1:5.) Some people will not understand why you are so kind, but they will be hungry for what you have. Some will even resent any expression of kindness toward them. This is why brotherly kindness must be an act of faith just like any of the other additives. Go ahead and obey God's commands to show kindness, for the Word will not fail.

That first group of believers must have shocked all the religious people when they began to sell their possessions and share what they had with those who were in need. (Acts 2:44-45.) God's love had come in and their lives were laid down for one another.

Add brotherly kindness and you will start using your faith to see opportunities to demonstrate God's kindness to others. The two go well together. In fact, they need each other. Coldness and indifference are not Christian traits. "And as ye would that men should do to you, do ye also to them likewise" (Luke 6:31).

"Give, and it shall be given unto you; good measure, pressed down, and shaken together, and running over, shall men give into your bosom. For with the same measure that ye mete withal it shall be measured to you again" (Luke 6:38). Although this passage can be used as a promise of financial blessing, the primary context of the teaching is love and kindness. As we give, it will be returned.

CHARITY (LOVE)

Love is the motivation for the God-kind of faith. It was the love God had for the people in the world that caused Him to plant a seed of faith in the earth—His only Son. It was love that moved Jesus to lay aside all the riches of glory to be born in an animal shelter and suffer in man's place on the cross.

"And though I have all faith, so that I could remove mountains, and have not charity, I am nothing" (I Corinthians 13:2). This verse does not say we should have love instead of faith. It says that **our faith must operate by love** or it will be empty. Do not go away from mountain-moving faith just because you do not feel capable of exercising mountain-moving love. Believe God for both. If He can give the faith, He can give the love.

"For in Christ Jesus neither circumcision availeth anything nor uncircumcision; but faith which worketh by love" (Galatians 5:6). Faith will not continue to operate without the power of love. It becomes empty and meaningless without God's love motivating and directing its power.

Faith and love are not in opposition to one another but rather they compliment each other. In Paul's letters faith and love are coupled together many times. (Galatians 5:6; Ephesians 6:23; Colossians 1:4; I Thessalonians 1:3; 3:6; 5:8; I Timothy 1:14; II Timothy 1:13; Philemon 5.) They are like two wings of an airplane. Each wing is separate as an individual, yet both are needed to fly.

Love keeps faith from becoming selfish because love always reaches outward either to God or man. (Matthew 22:37-39.) God does command us to love ourselves, but in doing so we are learning how to love our neighbor. Any way we look at it, the love we receive from God must never stop flowing. Its life-giving stream is too precious to be hoarded.

I have been healed many times by the power of God's love and faith. Today I am able to share this same message of God's healing power with others in need. Before we had heard the Word of God in this area, we had little to offer those in physical pain. At best we wished or hoped something would happen to relieve their agony. Perhaps our presence was an encouragement, but usually the conversation centered on trivial things that meant nothing and did very little to help. Thank God, today we can share the Word of God that promises healing for the believer, and many have received by faith.

Love and faith are both required to help meet the financial needs of others. A sincere love will move you to give beyond your natural abilities in faith that God will supply in a miraculous way. Big love needs big faith. In fact, **love will force your faith to grow.**

George Mueller had a great love for orphans and established a home for them in England. His intense love forced him to his knees daily to ask God for more and more provisions for the youngsters until the day came that the outreach was supporting hundreds of youth. He never asked a man for money, but fully trusted God. And God did not fail. Mueller's love gave him an object for his faith, and his faith touched God to provide for those he loved.

The story of Gethsemane, Calvary and an empty tomb, speaks of love and faith. Man had a need of salvation and God's love reached out to meet it. Jesus kept saying, "On the third day I will rise." After three days of darkness, faith won and Love arose. Now we live because He lives. It hurt and it cost, but God thought we were valuable enough to pay the supreme price for our redemption.

Love is the beginning and the ending—for God is love. (I John 4:16, Revelation 1:11.) LOVE NEVER FAILS. And if love is undergirding faith, then faith will not fail. (I Corinthians 13:8.) How we need to examine our hearts and make sure that we are being moved by love in our faith! Remember there are other voices in the world besides God's. The sheep follow the Good Shepherd for they know that His voice is filled with love. (John 10:27.)

Ask yourself these questions whenever you begin to exercise faith for some blessing:

Is it consistent with God's Word?

Will it bring glory to the Father and please Him?

Does it demonstrate my love for others?

These questions are not written to be a cut and dried formula, but rather to give you some guidelines to insure that your faith is working by love. (Galatians 5:6.) If you will abide in the Word and keep it with your whole heart, your desires will be godly. You will know by the witness of the Spirit what you should pray for in your life.

"But whoso keepeth his word, in him verily is the love of God perfected: hereby know we that we are in him" (I John 2:5).

"If ye keep my commandments, ye shall abide in my love; even as I have kept my Father's commandments, and abide in his love. This is my commandment. That ye love one another, as I have loved you. Herein is my Father glorified, that ye bear much fruit; so shall ye be my disciples" (John 15:10, 12, 8).

Conclusion

We have illustrated faith with the use of a machine to speak to a people well-acquainted with engines. Jesus spoke of leaven, tares, seed, vineyards, and sheep to explain the Kingdom. By taking the visible to illustrate the unseen, we can understand the deep mysteries of God.

Faith is much more than a machine, however. It is a life-giving force that brings God's love into human lives to save, heal, deliver, free, guide, and empower.

Tune up your faith and get all you can out of each part. Put the additives in and begin to thank God.

"For if ye do these things, ye shall never fall: For so an entrance shall be ministered unto you abundantly into the everlasting kingdom of our Lord and Savior Jesus Christ" (II Peter 1:10-11).

JESUS — THE WORD OF GOD

Matthew 4:4. Mark 4:3-25. John 1:1, 14; 6:63; 8:31-32; 14:6. Ephesians 6:17. II Timothy 3:16-17. I Thessalonians 2:13. Hebrews 4:12-13. I Peter 1:23; 2:2. II Peter 1:20-21. I John 5:7. Revelation 19:11-13. Isaiah 55:10-11. Jeremiah 1:12.

FAITH WORKS BY LOVE

Matthew 14:14. Galatians 5:6. I Corinthians 13:2,13. Ephesians 6:23. Colossians 1:4. I Thessalonians 1:3. II Thessalonians 1:3. II Timothy 1:13. Philemon 5. I Peter 4:8. II Peter 1:5-7. I John 2:4; 5:3. II John 6.

HEAR

Romans 10:17; Mark 4:23-25; Proverbs 4:20-21; John 6:45; 8:47; Revelation 1:3; Matthew 17:5; Luke 11:28; John 10:3-4; 12:48. Hebrews 3: 7-10.

(PERCEIVE, LEARN, LISTEN, UNDERSTAND, KNOW.)

BELIEVE — (TRUST, COMMIT, CHOOSE, AGREE, LEAN UPON)

Mark 11:24. John 3:16; 4:50; 5:24; 6:29; 20-29. Romans 10:8-10. II Corinthians 4:13. Galatians 3:22. Ephesians 1:19. I Thessalonians 2:13. I John 3:23.

PRAY — (ASK, REQUEST, COMMUNE, PETITION, SUPPLICATION)

Matthew 6:5-15. Mark 11:24. Luke 18:1. John 15:7; 16:23-24. Colosians 4:2. Hebrews 4:16. I John 3:21-22; 5:14-15.

RECEIVE — (ACCEPT, TAKE, EMBRACE, CLAIM, OBTAIN, HOLD, INHERIT)

Matthew 11:12; 21:22. Mark 4:20; 10:15; 11:24. John 1:12; 7:39; 16:24. Acts 2:38. Hebrews 4:16; 6:12; 10:35-36. Titus 1:9. I John 3:22.

CONFESS — (SPEAK, TALK, ACKNOWLEDGE, VOICE, EXPRESS)

Matthew 4:1-11; 8:8; 12:34-37. Mark 11:23. Romans 10:8-10. Ephesians 4:29. Titus 2:1,15. Philemon 1:6. Hebrews 4:14; 10:23. James 3:2-4. Revelation 12:11. Joshua 1:8. Psalm 19:14. Proverbs 6:2; 18:21.

MEDITATE — (PONDER, MUTTER, IMAGINE, STUDY, ABIDE, THINK UPON, DWELL, MURMER)

John 15:7. Philippians 4:8. Colossians 3:16, I Timothy 4:15, Joshua 1:8. Psalm 1:1-3; 19:14; 119:15,23,48,78,148.

PRAISE — (THANKSGIVING, WORSHIP, REJOICING, GLORIFY)

John 11:41; 15:11; 16:24. Acts 16:25-26. Romans 4:20-21. Philippians 1:4; 4:8. Colossians 4:2. I Thessalonians 5:16-18. Hebrews 13:15. James 1:2. I John 1:4. Joshua 6:20. II Chronicles 20:1-22. Psalm 100:4; 149.

ACT — (DO, OBEY, RESPOND, KEEP, WORK, LIVE, WALK, CONTINUE, PRACTICE)

Matthew 7:24-27. John 8:31-32; 14:15,21. Romans 6:17. II Corinthians 5:7. Philippians 2:12. Colossians 1:9-10. I Timothy 4:16. Titus 3:8. Hebrews 11:4,7,8,17. James 1:22-25; 2:16-26. I Peter 1:22. I John 1:7, 3:21,22,24; 5:2-3. Revelation 22:14. Joshua 1:8. I Samuel 15:22. Proverbs 4:4; 7:1-2.